THE ALL-TIME CLASSIC JOKE BOOK

Published in 2018 by Prion
An imprint of the Carlton Publishing Group
20 Mortimer Street, London W1T 3JW

10 9 8 7 6 5 4 3 2 1

A catalogue record for this book is available
from the British Library.

ISBN: 978 1 91161 012 0

Printed in Great Britain by CPI Group (UK) Ltd, Croydon CR0 4YY

THE ALL-TIME CLASSIC JOKE BOOK

ALL YOUR FAVOURITE JOKES, GAGS AND PUNS IN ONE HILARIOUS PLACE!

MIKE HASKINS

PRION

CONTENTS

ADULTERY

A woman arrives home after a shopping trip and is horrified to find her husband in bed with a pretty, firm young woman. She is about to storm out of the house, when her husband stops her by saying, "Honey, before you go, at least give me one chance to explain how on earth this happened!" The woman decides that she owes him this much at least, so stops to listen to his story. He begins, "Well I was driving home in the pouring rain, and I saw this poor thing at the bus stop, soaked. There's a bus strike on, so I offered her a lift, and it turned out that she was really hungry. So, I brought her home and gave her some of last night's leftovers that we didn't eat. I noticed her clothes were shabby, so I offered her that jumper that you wore once and didn't like and those trousers that don't fit you any more. I noticed her shoes were full of holes, so I gave her a pair of your shoes that you never liked, too. Anyway, so just as she was about to leave she asked me, 'And is there anything else that your wife doesn't use any more?' So here we are!"

Jake's friends always got mad at him because no matter how bad a situation was, he would always say, "It could be worse."

Finally, his friends decided to make up something that he couldn't say, "It could be worse" about. When they were playing golf one day Steve said to Jake, "Did you hear what happened to Fred?"

"No," said Jake.

"Fred came home Thursday and found his wife in bed with another man, killed them both and then turned the gun on himself."

"It could be worse," said Jake, predictably.

"How could it be any worse than that?" Steve asked.

"Well," Jake said, "if it had happened a day earlier, I'd be dead."

A woman was having a passionate affair with an inspector from a pest-control company. One afternoon, they were carrying on in the bedroom together when her husband arrived home quite unexpectedly. "Quick," said the woman to her lover. "Into the wardrobe!" And with that she pushed him into the wardrobe, stark naked. The husband, however, became suspicious and, after a search of the bedroom, discovered the man in the closet. "Who are you?" he asked him, with a snarl.

"I'm an inspector from Bugs-B-Gone," said the exterminator.

"What are you doing in there?" the husband asked.

"I'm investigating a complaint about moths," the man replied.

"So where are your clothes?" asked the husband.

The man looked down at himself and said, "Those little bastards."

A woman was in bed with her lover when she heard her husband opening the front door. "Hurry!" she said. "Stand in the corner!" She quickly rubbed baby oil all over him, and then she dusted him with talcum powder.

"Don't move until I tell you to," she whispered. "Just pretend you're a statue."

"What's this, honey?" the husband inquired as he entered the room.

"Oh, it's just a statue," she replied nonchalantly. "The Smiths bought one for their bedroom. I liked it so much, I got one for us, too."

No more was said about the statue, not even later that night when they went to sleep. Around 2am, the husband got out of bed, went to the kitchen and returned a while later with a sandwich and a glass of milk. "Here," he said to the statue, "eat something. I stood like an idiot at the Smiths' for three days, and nobody offered me as much as a glass of water."

A worried man calls up his best mate in a panic. "I really need your advice, pal. I'm desperate, and I don't know what to do."

His friend replies, "Sure, I'll try and help. What's wrong?"

The worried man explains: "For some time now, I've suspected that my wife may be cheating on me. You know the sort of thing; the phone rings, I answer, someone hangs up."

"That's terrible, mate," says his friend.

"That's not all," continues the worried man. "The other day, I picked up her mobile, just to see what time it was, and she went mental, screaming at me that I should never touch her phone again, and that I was checking up on her. So far I haven't confronted her about it. I sort of think, deep down, I don't really want to know the truth. But then, last night, she went out again, and I decided to check up on her. I hid behind my car, which I knew would give me a good view of the whole street. That way, I could see which car she got out of on her return. Anyway, it was while I was crouched behind my car that I noticed some rust around the rear wheel arch.

So, do you think I should take it into a body repair shop, or just buy some of that stuff from Halfords and try to sort it out myself?"

* * *

A man returns home a day early from a business trip and gets into a taxi at the airport after midnight. On the way back to his house, he asks the cabby if he would be a witness, as he suspects his wife is having an affair and he intends to catch her in the act.

For £100, the cabby agrees. They arrive at the house and the husband and cabby tiptoe into the bedroom. The husband switches on the lights, yanks the blanket back and there is his wife in bed with another man.

The husband immediately puts a gun to the naked man's head.

The wife shouts, "Don't do it! This man has been very generous! I lied when I told you I inherited money. He paid for the Porsche I bought for you, your United season ticket, the house at the lake and your golf club membership and green fees."

Shaking his head from side to side, the husband slowly lowers the gun and looks over at the cabbie and says, "What would you do?"

The cabby says, "I'd cover him up with that blanket before he catches a cold."

*   *   *

Every Wednesday morning for the past three years, Harry has woken up early, got his breakfast and headed off to the nearest lake for a whole day of fishing. This Wednesday, however, the weather is too bad. He's used to being cold and doesn't mind the wind, but today it would actually be dangerous for him to go out. As he walks out to his car in the drive, he realises that he's got to give up.

Silently, he comes back in and shakes off his soaking coat in the kitchen. He quietly sneaks back into the bedroom and, once there, he gets undressed and climbs into bed.

"Oh, hello, John," his wife says sleepily. "I didn't know if you'd come this morning with this weather. Would you believe my moron of a husband went fishing in this rain?"

AGEING

Two men in their nineties have been friends for decades, and after going through the war together, they now just meet a few times a week to play cards. One day, they're playing together when one of them suddenly puts down his cards.

"Listen, don't get mad at me, pal," he says. "I know we've been friends for years, but I realised the other day that I can't remember your name. I'm really embarrassed, but my memory is fading fast. Please remind me."

For three minutes the other old feller just glares back at his mate, shaking his head. Finally, he stirs.

"Look," he says, "how soon do you need to know?"

While out for a drive, an elderly couple stop at a service station for lunch. Back on the road afterwards, the elderly woman realises that she's left her glasses in the service station.

By then, they've travelled quite a distance and have to go even further before they can find a place to turn around.

The old feller moans and complains all the way back to the restaurant. He calls his wife every name he can think of, and when they finally arrive back at the service station and the woman gets out of the car to retrieve her glasses, the man yells to her, "And while you're in there, you might as well get my wallet, too!"

* * *

*What does a
75-year-old woman have
between her breasts that
a 25-year-old doesn't?
Her navel.*

* * *

Bert, 92, and Agnes, 89, are about to get married. They go for a stroll to discuss the wedding, and on the way, they pass a chemist. Bert suggests they go in.

Bert first asks the pharmacist, "Do you sell heart medication?"

Pharmacist: "Of course."

Bert: "How about medicine for circulation?"

Pharmacist: "All kinds."

Bert: "How about Viagra?"

Pharmacist: "Of course."

Bert: "Do you sell wheelchairs and walkers?"

Pharmacist: "We do – all speeds and sizes."

Bert: "That's brilliant! We'd like to use this shop for our wedding list, please."

Three sisters aged 92, 94 and 96 live in a house together. One night the 96-year-old runs a bath. She puts her foot in and pauses. She yells to the other sisters, "Was I getting in or out of the bath?"

The 94-year-old yells back, "I don't know. I'll come up and see."

She starts up the stairs and pauses, "Was I going up the stairs or down?" she shouts.

The 92-year-old is sitting at the kitchen table, having tea, listening to her sisters. She shakes her head and says, "I sure hope I never get that forgetful... knock on wood."

She then yells, "I'll come up and help both of you as soon as I see who's at the door."

* * *

Tom, an 80-year-old farmer, is at the doctor's telling him how he's going to marry a mail-order bride.

"How old is the new bride to be?" asks the Doc.

"She'll be twenty-one in November." Tom proudly proclaims.

Being the wise man that he is, the doctor realises that the sexual appetite of a young woman won't be satisfied by an 80-year-old man, and wanting his old patient's remaining years to be happy, the doctor tactfully suggests that Tom should consider getting a hired hand to help him out on the farm, knowing nature will take its own course.

About four months later, the doctor runs into Tom on the street.

"How's the new wife?" asks the doctor.

Tom proudly says, "She's pregnant."

The doctor, happy that his sage advice has worked out, continues, "And how's the hired hand?"

Without hesitating, Tom replies, "She's pregnant too!"

* * *

70-year-old George goes for his annual check-up. He tells the doctor that he feels fine, but often has to go to the bathroom during the night. Then he says: "But you know, Doc, I'm blessed. God knows my eyesight is going, so he puts on the light when I pee and turns it off when I'm done!"

A little later in the day, Dr Smith calls George's wife and says: "Your husband's test results were fine, but he said something strange that has been bugging me. He claims that God turns the light on and off for him when he uses the bathroom at night."

"That old fool!" Thelma exclaims. "He's been peeing in the refrigerator again!"

* * *

Morris and his wife, Esther, went to the funfair every year. And every year, Morris would say, "Esther, I'd like to ride in that helicopter."

Esther always replied, "Yes, it looks fun, Morris, but that helicopter ride is £50 – and £50 is £50."

One year later, Esther and Morris went to the fair again.

Morris said, "Esther, I'm 85 years old. If I don't ride that helicopter now, I might never get another chance."

Esther replied, "That's all very well, Morris, but that helicopter ride is £50 – and £50 is £50."

The pilot overheard the couple. He said, "Folks, I'll make you a deal. I'll take both of you for a ride. If you can stay quiet for the entire ride and not say a word, I won't charge you. But if you say one word, it's £50."

Morris and Esther agreed and up they went. The pilot did all kinds of fancy manoeuvres, but not a word was heard. He did his daredevil tricks over and over again, but still not a word. When they landed, the pilot turned to Morris and said, "Blimey! I did everything I could to get you to yell out, but you didn't. I'm impressed!"

Morris replied, "Well, I was going to say something when Esther fell out halfway through, but £50 is £50."

* * *

An elderly gentleman had serious hearing problems for a number of years. He went to the doctor and was fitted with a set of hearing aids that allowed him to hear 100 per cent.

A month later, the gentleman went back for a check-up. The doctor said, "Your hearing's perfect. Your family must be really pleased for you."

The gentleman replied, "Oh, I haven't told my family yet. I just sit around and listen to the conversations. I've changed my will three times so far!"

Two old men are sitting outside the town hall where a flower show is in progress. One complains, "Cripes, life is boring. We never have any fun! For £10, I'll streak naked through the flower show!" "You're on!" the other geriatric shouts.

The first old man fumbles out of his clothes and streaks through the hall. Waiting outside, his friend hears a commotion, followed by applause. Then, the naked old man bursts through the door, surrounded by a cheering crowd.

"How did it go?" asks the friend.

"Great!" says the wrinkled streaker. "I won first prize for dried arrangement!"

* * *

A local reporter goes to an old people's home to interview an ageing but legendary explorer. After hearing many incredible tales, he asks the old man to tell him about the most frightening experience he's ever had on his travels.

"Once, I was hunting tigers in the jungles of India. I was on a narrow path, and my native guide was behind me, carrying my rifle. Just then, the largest tiger I've ever seen leapt out in front of us. I turned around for my weapon only to find that the native had fled. The tiger pounced at me with a mighty 'Roarrrr!' I'm sorry to say I soiled myself."

The reporter says, "Sir, don't be embarrassed. Under those circumstances anyone would have done the same."

"No, not then," the old man replies. "Just now, when I went 'Roarrrr!'"

* * *

Three old men are at the hospital for a memory test. "What's three times three?" the doctor asks the first old man.

"Two hundred and seventy-four," he replies. "What's three times three?" the doctor asks the second old man. "Tuesday," he replies.

The doctor quickly realises he's in for a very long morning. He turns to the third old man and asks, "OK, your turn. What's three times three?"

"Nine," he replies.

"Yes!" exclaims the doctor. "How did you get that?"

"Easy. I just subtracted 274 from Tuesday."

One night, an old lady comes home from bingo to find her 92 year-old-husband in bed with another woman. She becomes violent and ends up pushing him off the balcony of their 20th-floor assisted living apartment, killing him instantly. Brought before the court on a charge of murder, she is asked by the judge if she has anything to say in her own defence.

"Yes, Your Honour. I figured that at 92, if he could have sex, he could fly."

* * *

A group of OAPs were sitting around talking about their various ailments.

"My arms are so weak, I can hardly hold this cup of coffee," said one.

"Yes, I know," replied another. "My cataracts are so bad I can't even see my coffee."

"I can't turn my head because of the arthritis in my neck," said a third, to which several nodded weakly in agreement.

"My blood pressure pills make me dizzy," another went on.

"I guess that's the price we pay for getting old," winced an old man.

There was a moment of silence. "Well, it's not that bad," said one woman cheerfully.

"Thank God we can all still drive!"

* * *

At 78, Raymond is still a very good golf player. His stance is perfect, his swing marvellous. He's got only one problem: he can't see very well any more. More often than not, he can't really see where his ball is going, and it's starting to be a real problem. Irritated at having to ask for help, he nonetheless asks his old friend John if he wouldn't mind giving him a hand.

"I don't want any advice or anything," Raymond warns gruffly. "All I want is you to tell me where the ball goes, OK?"

John accepts and off they go one day, shuffling slowly in the morning air to the first hole.

Raymond peers ahead, manages to see the little flag way off in the distance and swings. The ball, as usual now, travels far too fast for him to see it.

"Can you see it?" he asks John.

"Oh yes, no problem. Beautiful shot," John congratulates his friend.

Raymond waits a minute and then asks, "Right. Now. Where is it?"

John is silent for a while, then replies, "I forgot."

* * *

A man and a woman are sitting outside their old folks' home talking of the old days. All of a sudden, an ice cream van pulls up at the gate with the tune playing. The woman says, "I'd love an ice cream, you know," to which the man replies, "Would you like me to get you one?" "Don't bother", the old dear says, "by the time you get to the van you'll never remember what I wanted anyway." "Don't be silly," says the man, "I won't forget. Now, come on: what do you want?" "Well, OK, then," says the woman, "I'll have a double-scoop of strawberry with chocolate sauce, nuts and a flake on top." "A double-scoop of strawberry with chocolate sauce, nuts and a flake on top coming right up," says the man and off he goes. Five minutes later he comes back carrying four hot dogs and two large

Cokes. "Oh, my God," says the woman, "I knew I shouldn't have trusted you – where's the gravy?"

* * *

A tour bus driver is driving a bus full of OAPs on holiday, when a little old lady taps him on his shoulder. She offers him a handful of almonds, which he gratefully munches down. After about 15 minutes, she taps him on his shoulder again and hands him another handful of almonds. She repeats this gesture about eight times. At the ninth time, he asks the little old lady why they don't eat the almonds themselves? She explains that because of their false teeth, they can't chew them.

"Why do you buy them then?" the puzzled driver asks. The old lady answers, "We just love the chocolate around them."

ANIMALS

A cat from Oxford University and a cat from Paris University had a boat race on the Thames.

To make things fair, each was rowing the same kind of boat with the same kind of oars, and each cat wore the same number. The Oxford cat wore the number One-Two-Three and the Paris cat wore the French version, Un-Deux-Trois.

They started off neck and neck, with One-Two-Three rowing hard and Un-Deux-Trois staying level.

Then, One-Two-Three shot into the lead as the Un-Deux-Trois cat sank.

* * *

What's the last thing to go through an insect's mind when it flies into a car? Its bum!

* * *

Why do gorillas have big nostrils? Because they have big fingers.

* * *

It was a sad day when the old gorilla at the zoo
finally died. He was a great attraction; he always
made the children laugh and everyone loved him.
Unfortunately, the zoo couldn't afford to buy a
new gorilla, but the head keeper had a bit of a
brainwave. His brother-in-law was an out-of-work
actor, so he asked him to dress in a gorilla suit and
go in the gorilla's cage.

"No one will know you're not a real gorilla," said
the head keeper.

"No one gets close enough. All you have to do is
lark around like the other gorilla did, the children
will laugh and everyone will love you."

So, the actor put on the gorilla suit and got in
the cage. He larked around and made the children
laugh. Then he larked around some more, climbing
up the bars of his cage. Everyone loved him.

Unfortunately, he larked around a bit too much
and fell out of his cage into the tiger's cage. The
tiger immediately leapt on him.

"HELP!" screamed the actor. "HELP ME!"

"SHUT UP!" said the tiger, "or we'll both be
sacked!"

* * *

A gorilla walks into a bar and orders a pint of lager. The barman charges him five quid and, after looking at him for a while, says, "Do you know, you're the first gorilla we've had in here for ages?"

"I'm not bloody surprised," replies the gorilla, "at a fiver a pint."

* * *

A man who hates his wife's cat decides to get rid of it by driving it to the next town and leaving it there. But when he gets home, the cat's already back. The next day, he drops the cat off even further away, but the same thing happens. Finally, the man dumps the cat hundreds of miles away. Hours later, the man calls home to his wife: "Honey, is the cat there?"

"Yes," she says.

"Can you put him on? I'm lost."

* * *

What do you do if you are allergic to biting insects? DON'T BITE ANY!

* * *

A man takes his Rottweiler to the vet.

"My dog's cross-eyed," the man says. "Is there anything you can do for him?"

"Well," says the vet, "let's have a look at him."

The vet picks the dog up and examines his eyes, then checks his teeth. Finally he says, "I'm going to have to put him down."

The man is stricken. "What? Just because he's cross-eyed?"

"No," says the vet. "Because my arms are really starting to hurt."

* * *

Two turtles are camping. After four days hiking, they realize they've left behind a bottle opener for their beer.

The first turns to the second and says, "You've got to go back or else we've got no lager."

"No way," says the second turtle. "By the time I get back, you'll have eaten all the food."

The first turtle replies, "I promise I won't, OK? Just hurry."

Nine full days pass and there's still no sign of the second turtle, so the first finally cracks and digs into a sandwich. Suddenly the second turtle pops out from behind a rock and yells.

"I knew it! I'm definitely not going now!"

A man walks into a bar. He has a monkey with him. The man orders a drink, and while he drinks it, the monkey runs wild around the whole bar, annoying everyone including the man. While the man is drinking, the monkey runs up to the pool table, climbs up a cue, grabs the cue ball, sticks it in his mouth and swallows it.

The barkeep walks up to the man and says, "Did you see what your bloody monkey just did?"

"No, what did the little prick do this time?" replies the man.

"He just swallowed the cue ball from my pool table, that's what he just did," says the barkeep, angrily.

"Well, hopefully it'll kill the little bastard because I'm sick of him and his little tricks," says the man. He then finishes his drink and leaves.

A couple of weeks later the same man enters the bar with the same monkey. He orders the same drink, and the monkey runs wild around the whole bar, same as last time. While the man is drinking, the monkey finds some peanuts on a tray on the bar. He picks one up, sticks it up his backside, takes it out again and eats it. The bartender finds this disgusting, so he walks up to the man again.

"Did you see what your bloody monkey just did?"

"No, what did the little prick do this time?" sighs the man.

"He just stuck a peanut up his backside, took it out and ate it," says the barkeep.

"Well, what do you expect?" says the monkey's owner. "Ever since he ate that sodding cue ball, he has to measure everything first!"

* * *

Two chimps in a bath.
One says, "Oh, oh, ah, ah, ee, ee!"
The other one says,
"Put some cold water in then."

* * *

*Which side of a duck has
the most feathers?
The outside*

Two caterpillars are sitting on a leaf when a butterfly flutters past them.

One caterpillar turns to the other and says, "You'd never get me up in one of those."

* * *

Two campers are walking through the woods, when a huge brown bear suddenly appears in the clearing about 50 feet in front of them. The bear sees the campers and begins to head toward them. The first guy drops his backpack, digs out a pair of trainers and frantically begins to put them on.

The second bloke says, "What are you doing? Trainers won't help you outrun that bear."

"I don't need to outrun the bear," the first bloke says. "I just need to outrun you."

* * *

A man was on holiday in Kenya. While he was walking through the bush, he came across an elephant standing with one leg raised in the air. The elephant seemed distressed, so the man approached it, very carefully. He got down on one knee and inspected the elephant's foot. There was a large thorn deeply embedded in the bottom of the foot. As carefully and as gently as he could, he removed the thorn, and the elephant gingerly put down its foot. The elephant turned to face the man and with a rather stern look on its face, stared at him.

For a good ten minutes, the man stood frozen, thinking of nothing else but being trampled. Eventually the wrinkly-skinned mammal trumpeted loudly, turned and walked away.

Years later, the man was walking through a zoo with his son. As they approached the elephant enclosure, one of the creatures turned and walked over to where they were standing at the rail. It stared at him, and the man couldn't help wondering if this was the same elephant. After a while it trumpeted loudly, then it continued to stare at him. The man summoned up his courage, climbed over the railing and made his way into the enclosure. He walked right up to the elephant and stared back in wonder. Suddenly the elephant trumpeted again, wrapped its trunk around one of the man's legs and swung him wildly back and forth along the railing, killing him.

Probably wasn't the same elephant.

* * *

A man walks into a pub holding a turtle. The turtle has two bandaged legs, a black eye and his shell is held together with duct tape. The landlord asks, "What's wrong with your turtle?"

"Nothing," the man responds. "This turtle's very fast. Have your dog stand at the end of the bar. Then go and stand at the other end of the room and call him. Before that mutt reaches you, my turtle will be there."

So the landlord, wanting to see this, sets his dog at one side of the room. Then he goes to the other side and calls him. Suddenly, the guy picks up his bandaged turtle and throws it across the room, narrowly missing the landlord and smashing it into the wall.

"Told you!"

*What has two grey
legs and two brown legs?
An elephant with diarrhoea.*

* * *

*What's worse than
a giraffe with a sore neck?
A millipede with
in-growing toenails*

* * *

A burglar breaks into a house and creeps into a room
with no lights on. He walks into the room and hears
a voice which says, "Jesus is watching you."

The thief turns around and, in a dark corner
of the room, he sees a parrot. As he creeps over to
shut the bird up, the parrot shrieks again, "Jesus is
watching you."

The annoyed burglar looks at the parrot and asks,
"What's your name?" The parrot replies, "Clarence."

The burglar laughs and, as he's about to throttle

the bird, says, "That's a stupid name for a parrot. What idiot called you that?"

The parrot replies, "The same idiot who decided to call the Rottweiler Jesus."

* * *

A woman's dishwasher breaks down, so she calls a repairman.

Since she has to go to work the next day, she tells the repairman, "I'll leave the key under the mat. Fix the dishwasher, leave the bill on the counter, and I'll send you a cheque in the post. Oh, by the way, don't worry about my bulldog. He won't bother you. But, whatever you do, do not, under any circumstances, talk to my parrot! I repeat, do not talk to my parrot!"

When the repairman arrives at the woman's apartment the following day, he discovers the biggest, meanest-looking bulldog he has ever seen. But, just as the woman warns, the dog just lays there on the carpet watching the repairman go about his work. The parrot, however, is driving the man nuts the whole time with its incessant yelling, cursing and name-calling.

Finally, the repairman can contain himself no longer and yells, "Shut up, you stupid ugly bird!"

The parrot replies, "Get him, Spike."

* * *

A local business is looking for office help. They put a sign in the window, stating: "HELP WANTED. Must be able to type, must be good with a computer and must be bilingual."

A short time afterwards, a dog trots up to the window and goes inside. He looks at the receptionist and wags his tail, then walks over to the sign, looks at it and whines. Getting the idea, the receptionist gets the office manager.

The manager says, "I can't hire you. The sign says you have to be able to type."

With that, the dog jumps down, goes to the typewriter and proceeds to type out a perfect letter.

The manager is stunned, but tells the dog, "The sign also says you have to be good with a computer."

The dog jumps down again and goes to the computer, where it enters and executes a spreadsheet perfectly.

By this time the manager is totally dumbfounded. He looks at the dog and says, "I realise that you are a very intelligent dog and have some interesting abilities. However, I still can't give you the job. You have to be bilingual."

The dog looks at the manager calmly and says, "Meow!"

* * *

One day, a little 5'1" guy walks into a pub and asks, "Excuse me, does anyone here own a big Rottweiler?"

A 7'1" man stands up and says, "That's Tyson. He's mine, why?"

"I think my dog has killed yours," says the pipsqueak, eyeing the big guy nervously.

"I don't believe it," says the hard man. "What breed is your dog? Doberman? Pit Bull?"

"No, it's a Chihuahua," says the man.

"How can a Chihuahua kill a Rottweiler?" asks the owner.

"It got stuck in your dog's throat," replies the little feller.

* * *

A man follows a woman with a parrot out of a cinema, stops her and says, "I'm sorry to bother you, but I couldn't help noticing that your bird seemed to understand the film. He cried at the right parts, and he laughed at the jokes. Don't you find that unusual?"

"I do indeed," she replies. "He hated the book."

* * *

What do you call an insect that flies around a lampshade at 180mph? Stirling Moth.

* * *

A woman is taking a stroll through the woods when a little white duck, covered in filth, crosses her path.

"Let me clean you," the woman says, taking a tissue from her purse.

The woman walks on a little further and encounters another duck, also with muck all over it. Again, she produces a tissue and cleans the bird. Afterwards, she hears a voice from the bushes.

"Excuse me, madam," it says. "Do you have any more tissues?"

"No!" the woman replies, offended.

"All right," the voice says. "I'll just have to use another duck, then."

* * *

One day, in the shark-infested waters of the Caribbean, two prawns called Justin and Christian are discussing the pressures of being a preyed-upon prawn.

"I hate being a prawn," says Justin, "I wish I were a shark."

Suddenly a mysterious cod appears. "Your wish is granted," he says.

Instantly Justin becomes a shark. Horrified, Christian swims away, afraid his former friend might eat him. As time passes, Christian continues to avoid Justin, leaving the shrimp-turned predator lonely and frustrated. So when he bumps into the cod again, he begs the mysterious fish to change him back. Lo and behold, Justin is turned back into a prawn. With tears of joy in his tiny little eyes, he swims back to the reef to seek out Christian.

As he approaches, he shouts out, "It's me, Justin, your old friend. I've changed... I've found Cod. I'm a prawn again, Christian."

* * *

Feeling uncertain about his love life, a frog calls up a psychic hotline.

"I can see that you're going to meet a beautiful young girl who will want to know everything about you," the psychic tells the frog.

"That's great," the frog says. "Will I meet this babe at a party?"

"No," the psychic says. "In her biology class next term."

A woman walks into the kitchen to find her husband stalking around with a fly-swatter.

"What are you doing?" she asks.

"Hunting flies," he replies.

"Oh. Killed any?" she enquires.

"Three males and two females," the husband responds.

Intrigued, she asks, "How can you tell?"

"Easy," the husband replies. "Three were on a beer can and the other two were on the phone."

* * *

A little old lady had two monkeys for years. One day, one of them died of natural causes. Overcome with grief, the second monkey passed away two days later. Not knowing what to do with the remains, she finally decided to take them to the taxidermist and have them stuffed.

After telling the owner of her wishes, he asked her, "Do you want them mounted?"

"No. Holding hands will be fine," she said, blushing.

* * *

What animal has four legs, hooves and stripes all over? A horse in his pyjamas

A guy walks into a bar with a weird dog on a leash: he's stumpy-legged, pink, and doesn't have a tail.

The barman spots him and says, with a greedy look in his eyes, "I bet my Rottweiler would beat the heck out of your dog, mate."

A bet of £50 is duly made, but out in the yard the Rottweiler gets mauled to pieces.

A customer, surveying the scene, raises the stakes: he's got a pit bull that will tear this weird dog to pieces, but the bet has to be £100. Another trip to the yard and, when it's all over, there are bits of pit bull terrier all over the place.

The customer, dismayed, pays up and says, "Say, what breed is this dog anyway?"

The owner says, "Until I cut his tail off and painted him pink, he was the same breed as every other alligator."

* * *

What do you get if you cross a giraffe with a porcupine? A five-metre-high walking toilet brush

* * *

A man walks into a bar with his dog.

"Hold on. You can't bring that dog in here!" says the barman.

The guy, without missing a beat, says, "This is my guide dog."

"Oh, man," the bartender says, "I'm sorry. Here, the first one's on me."

The man takes his drink and goes to a table near the door.

Another guy walks into the bar with a Chihuahua. The first guy sees him, stops him and says, "You can't bring that dog in here unless you tell him it's a guide dog."

The second man gratefully thanks the first man and continues to the bar. He asks for a drink.

The bartender says, "Hey, you can't bring that dog in here!"

The second man replies, "This is my seeing-eye dog."

The bartender says, "No, I don't think so. Since when do they have Chihuahuas as guide dogs?"

The man pauses for half a second and replies, "What? They gave me a Chihuahua?"

* * *

A blind man was waiting at the zebra crossing when his guide dog started peeing on his leg. Unfazed, the blind man reached into his pocket and took out a dog biscuit to give to the dog.

A pedestrian waiting with him on the pavement witnessed the incident, approached the blind man and said, "This is very decent of you. You're a very tolerant person, especially after what the dog did to you."

"Not really," replies the blind man. "I'm just checking where his mouth is so I can kick him in the balls."

* * *

Two flies land on a steaming heap of manure.
The first lifts his leg and farts.
The other fly says, "Jesus, Jim. I'm trying to eat."

Why do female black widow spiders kill their partners after mating? To stop the snoring before it starts.

* * *

A scientist is studying frogs in a Brazilian swamp and is quite puzzled. The frog population is dwindling, although the males look healthy enough. After a week of research, he realises there's something in the water that prevents the frogs from staying together long enough to copulate, as if it were too oily or something. He goes back to his camp and, with his assistant, concocts some potion, which he puts in a large aquarium together with water samples from the swamp. They're at it for another week before stumbling upon the right combination: some algae extract, chemicals of some sort and a pinch of salt.

As they watch the frogs happily reproducing, the scientist remarks, "Who would have guessed? They need monosodium glue to mate.

* * *

It is a very important race for this jockey, and he's unlucky enough to have to ride a new horse he's never ridden before.

"Don't worry about it," the trainer tells him. "He's very good, honest. He's got a little quirk, though. Just before you jump, you'll have to shout, 'One, two, three, jump!' and you'll be fine."

The jockey doesn't have time to voice his disbelief because he and his horse are called to the line. Off they go, and here comes the first fence. The jockey ignores the trainer's advice, and the horse goes crashing into the jump, sending the jockey head over heels.

Quickly he remounts and off they go. This time, though, the jockey does some thinking and realises that acting a bit ridiculous is better than losing the race. So, when it's time to jump again, he whispers, "One, two, three, jump!" into the horse's ear… to no avail. The horse goes crashing into the jump and sends him flying again.

Pissed off and bruised, the jockey remounts, and this time at the third fence shouts loudly, "One, two, three, JUMP!" It's a miracle; the horse gracefully clears the fence and performs a fantastic jump. It's far too late for the jockey, though, who finishes the race well behind the rest of the field.

Dismounting and leading the horse by the bridle, he goes to the trainer. "What's the matter with this damn horse?" he explodes. "Is he deaf?"

"No, he's not deaf, you idiot, he's blind!" he replies.

* * *

Two cows were standing in a field.
One cow says to the other, "Moooooo."
The other says, "I was just going to say that."

* * *

Mama Weevil gave birth to two identical twin weevils. They grew up together, but there came a time when they had to discover the world on their own. Tearfully they separated, each to go its own weevil way.

One was very successful in Hollywood, got tons of girlfriends and money, while the other didn't have much luck in its life and ended up broke, alone and miserable. He was therefore known as the lesser of two weevils.

* * *

A non-too-bright zebra escaped from a zoo and ended up in a field full of cows.

He walked up to one and said, "Hi there. What do you do around here then?"

"I eat grass all day and get milked morning and night," replied the cow.

"Oh," the zebra said. He walked idly about and met another cow.

"Hi there! Say, what do you do around here then?" he asked again.

"I eat grass all day and get milked morning and night," replied the cow.

The zebra nodded, pleased by the quietness and the sense of purpose of the cows' life, then walked over to a bull. "Hello," he said. 'What do you do around here?"

The bull looked him up and down and said, "Get those pyjamas off and I'll show you."

A man is having a nap in a deckchair in the garden, when a scraping sound wakes him up. In horror, he sees that his dog is dragging a dead rabbit. And not just any old dead rabbit, but the neighbour's daughter's rabbit, a rabbit she's loved since she was a toddler.

He quickly shoos the dog away and picks up the dead rabbit. "Maybe if I clean it up a bit I can put it back in its cage and no one will say anything. They'll think he died there," he reasons, in his half-awake state. He goes into the garage and cleans up the dead rabbit as well as he can, removing soil from the fur and checking that there aren't any tooth marks on it. He then sneaks into the neighbour's garden and carefully places the animal back in its cage. When all this is done, he returns to his deckchair, waiting for the neighbours to come back from shopping.

After an hour or so, he hears the neighbour's car pulling into the drive. So far so good. Maybe his ruse has worked, and no one will think his dog killed the rabbit.

Then, suddenly, a piercing cry: "Daddy!"

"Here we go," he thinks, saddened by the anguish he can hear in the neighbour's daughter's cry.

"I can't believe it!" he hears the neighbour's dad exclaim in outrage. "What kind of a sick weirdo would dig up a little girl's dead rabbit and put it back in its cage?"

* * *

What goes "Oooooooooooo"?
A cow with no lips.

* * *

A duck enters a grocery store and says to the man behind the counter, "Do you have any beer?"

"I'm sorry, but this is a grocery store. We're not licensed to sell beer here."

The duck leaves, but comes back the next day.

"Do you have any beer?" he asks.

"I told you yesterday! We don't sell beer here! This is a grocery store! If you come here again asking for beer, I'll nail your feet to the floor!"

The duck leaves, but comes back the next day.

"Got any nails?'

The shop owner says, "No."

"Got any beer?"

* * *

An old man walks into a bar using a cane and carrying a crocodile.

The barman says, 'Sorry, mate, no animals allowed in here – especially dangerous ones like that.'

The man says, 'Oh, go on: my croc can do a fantastic trick and it'll have people coming from miles around to see it. Let me show you.'

'Well, OK then,' says the barman, 'but if I think it's crap I'm going to chuck the pair of you out.'

So the old man says something to the croc, who gets up on his hind legs and opens his mouth. The man then drops his trousers and puts his pecker into the croc's mouth. The croc shuts its mouth tight around his pecker. The crowd in the bar all gasp out loud. But then the man picks up his cane and raps the croc's head with it three times – tap, tap, tap! The croc opens its mouth and the man's pecker is there – still attached – without even a scratch on it. Everyone in the bar starts clapping and cheering the old man.

'Now,' says the man looking around the bar, 'Does anybody else think they're up to this fantastic trick? Would anyone else like a go?'

There is silence and all the men look to the floor. Suddenly an old lady pipes up, 'I'll have a try, but you only need to hit me on the head once!'

* * *

Deep in the forest, a tortoise was slowly padding towards a tall tree. Ever so slowly she started climbing the tree. After a few days of this, she managed to climb high enough to reach the lowest branch, but it was apparently not high enough, as she carried on upwards.

It took her a week to reach a suitable branch and then another three days to arrive at the end of the branch. Once there, she took a deep breath and hurled herself forward, instantly falling like a brick all the way down, finishing her trip with a thud in the humus.

A couple of birds had been watching the whole process for a week and the male bird turned to his mate and chirped: 'Dear, I know how much this will upset you, but we'll have to tell her she's adopted.'

* * *

A frog goes into a London bank and approaches the teller. He can see from her nameplate that the teller's name is Patricia Whack.

He says, "Ms. Whack, I'd like to get a loan to buy a boat and go on a long vacation."

Patti looks at the frog in disbelief and asks how much he wants to borrow. The frog says £30,000. The teller asks his name, and the frog says that his name is Kermit Jagger and that it's OK, he knows the bank manager. Patti explains that £30,000 is a substantial amount of money, and that he will need to secure the loan. She asks if he has anything he can use as collateral.

The frog says, "Sure. I have this," and he produces a tiny pink porcelain elephant, about half an inch tall. It's bright pink and perfectly formed, but of no obvious visible value.

Very confused, Patti explains that she'll have to consult with the manager and disappears into a back office. She finds the manager and reports:

"There's a frog called Kermit Jagger out there who claims to know you, and he wants to borrow £30,000. He wants to use this as collateral," she says, holding up the tiny pink elephant. "I mean, what the heck is this?"

The bank manager looks back at her and says, "It's a knick-knack, Patti Whack. Give the frog a loan. His old man's a Rolling Stone!"

* * *

What do giraffes have that no other animal can possibly have? **Baby giraffes!**

* * *

A team of elephants had agreed to play a game of football against a team of ants. Things were going well for the ants – more agile and nimble than the elephants – when the referee whistled loudly.

Everybody from both teams gathered around the remains of an unfortunate ant, now completely squashed to bits on the pitch.

"There you are," an ant complained bitterly. "You just can't trust the big people to play fair!"

"I didn't want this to happen," the elephant said guiltily. "I just wanted to trip him over."

* * *

A duck walks into a bar and orders a pint of beer. Amazed, the bartender says, "Hey, you can talk!"

"Sure, pal," says the duck. "Now can I get that drink?"

Shaking his head, the barman serves the duck a pint and asks him what he's doing in the area.

"I work on the building site across the street," says the duck.

"You should join the circus," says the barman. "You could make a mint."

"The circus?" the duck replies. "What the hell would the circus want with a bricklayer?"

* * *

A tiny zoo in Suffolk is given a very rare species of gorilla by an eccentric explorer. After a couple of weeks, the gorilla starts to go wild: it won't eat, can't sleep, becomes violent and causes all sorts of problems. The zoo owner calls the vet in who determines that the gorilla is a female and, what's more, she's on heat. The only way to calm her down is to have someone mate with her. Sadly, there are no other gorillas of her species in captivity, so another solution will have to be found. It is then that the owner remembers Jimmy, the cage cleaner. Jimmy is a bit dumb, but he has a reputation for having sex with anything, so the owner decides to offer him a proposition: would he like to have sex with the gorilla for £500? Jimmy says he's interested, but that he'll need the night to think it over. The next day, he says he'd be willing and that he'd accept the offer, but only if the owner meets three conditions.

"First," he says, "I don't want to kiss her on the lips."

The owner says that's fine.

"Second," Jimmy says, "You must never, ever tell anyone about this."

"That's fine," the owner says again.

"And third," says Jimmy, "I'm going to need another week to come up with the money."

* * *

A man is sitting in an airliner which is about to take off, when a man with a Labrador retriever occupies the empty seats alongside. The Lab is situated in the middle, and the first man is looking quizzically at the dog while the second man explains that they work for the airline.

The airline rep said, "Don't mind Sniffer. He is a sniffing dog, the best there is. I'll show you once we get airborne and I put him to work."

The plane takes off and levels out when the handler says to the first man, "Watch this." He tells the dog, "Sniffer, search."

Sniffer jumps down, walks along the aisle and sits next to a woman for a few seconds. It then returns to its seat and puts one paw on the handler's arm, who says, "Good boy."

The airline rep turns to the first man and says, "That woman is in possession of marijuana, so I'm making a note of this and her seat number, so the police can apprehend her on arrival."

"Fantastic!" replies the first man.

Once again the rep sends Sniffer to search the

aisles. The Lab sniffs about, sits down beside a man for a few seconds, returns to its seat and places two paws on the handler's arm.

The airline rep says, "That man is carrying cocaine, so again I'm making a note of this and the seat number."

* * *

"I like it!" says the first man.

A third time the rep sends Sniffer to search the aisles. Sniffer goes up and down the plane and after a while sits down next to someone. He then comes racing back, jumps up onto his seat and craps all over the place. The first man is really grossed out by this behaviour from a supposedly well-trained sniffing dog and asks, "What's going on?"

The handler nervously replies, "He just found a bomb!"

A ventriloquist is on a walking holiday in Wales and getting pretty bored. During one of his walks he stumbles across a farm and there, leaning on a gate, is a farmer, so the ventriloquist decides to have a bit of fun.

"Hey, cool dog you have here, sir. Mind if I speak to him?"

"My dog doesn't talk," the farmer says, surprised.

"Hey, dog, how's it going?" the ventriloquist asks the dog.

"Doin' alright," the dog says.

The farmer stares at his dog in total disbelief, as he can't believe man's best friend can talk.

"This is your owner, right?" the prankster asks the dog, pointing at the farmer.

"Yep," says the dog.

"How is he treating you?"

"Real good. He walks me twice a day, feeds me great food and takes me to the lake once a week to play."

The farmer is still shocked, starting to feel bad over rubbing his dog's nose into his own poop after last week's potty incident.

"Mind if I talk to your horse?" the ventriloquist then asks.

"Hey?" blurts the farmer. "My horse doesn't talk." The ventriloquist approaches the horse:

"Hey, horse, how's it going?"

"Cool," says the horse.

"Is this your owner?"

"Yep," says the horse.

"How's he treating you?"

"Pretty good, thanks for asking. He rides me regularly, brushes me down often and keeps me in the barn to protect me from the elements."

By this time, the farmer is completely amazed and his eyes are bulging out of their sockets.

The ventriloquist approaches the gate and says, "Mind if I talk to your sheep?"

The farmer coughs loudly and says quickly, "Sheep lie!"

CHILDREN

The class was talking about Santa Claus in the run-up to Christmas and teacher asked if anyone knew how many reindeer pulled Santa's sleigh.

"Two!" said one small boy.

"Only two?" said teacher. "Are you sure?"

"Sure I'm sure," said the boy. "It says so in the song: Rudolph the red-nosed reindeer, had a very shiny nose, and if you ever saw it, you would even say it glowed. Olive, the other reindeer..."

* * *

A little girl asked her dad what the time was.

Her father proudly pulled out the large, heavy, gold pocket watch his grandfather had given him ... and promptly dropped it on the floor.

"Oh, dear!" said the girl as her father picked up the watch. "Did your watch stop when it hit the floor, Dad?"

"Of course it did!" said her father. "Did you think it would go straight through?"

* * *

Dad was happy typing away on his computer and didn't notice his six-year-old daughter sneaking up behind him. Then she turned and ran into the kitchen, squealing to the rest of the family, "I know Daddy's password! I know Daddy's password!"

"What is it?" her sister asked eagerly.
Proudly she replied, "Asterisk, asterisk, asterisk, asterisk, asterisk!"

* * *

A woman gets on a bus and immediately becomes involved in an argument with the driver when he calls her baby ugly. She pays her fare and storms off to get a seat, visibly upset.

The man next to her asks "What's the matter, love?"

"It's that bloody driver. I've never been so insulted in all my life," she replies.

"OK," says the man. "You go down there and sort him out. I'll look after your monkey."

* * *

One day at school, a teacher asks her class to write a sentence about a public servant, and little Jonny writes, "The fireman came down the ladder pregnant."

When she gets around to marking Jonny's answer, the teacher takes him aside to correct him. "Don't you know what pregnant means?" she asks.

"Sure," says Jonny. "It means carrying a child."

* * *

A little girl walks in to the lounge one Sunday morning where her Dad is reading the paper.

"Where does poo come from?" she asks.

Father, feeling a little perturbed that his five-year-old daughter is already asking difficult questions, thinks for a moment and says, "Well, you know we just ate breakfast?"

"Yes," replies the girl.

"Well, the food goes into our tummies, and our bodies take out all the good stuff, and then whatever's left over comes out of our bottoms when we go to the toilet. That's poo."

The little girl looks perplexed, and stares at him in stunned silence for a few seconds and asks, "And Tigger?"

* * *

How do you stop a kid wetting the bed? Give him an electric blanket.

* * *

Little David was in his primary class, when the teacher asked the children what their fathers did for a living. All the typical answers came up: fireman, policeman, salesman. David was being uncharacteristically quiet, so the teacher asked him about his father.

"My father's an exotic dancer in a gay cabaret and he takes off all his clothes in front of other men," he replied.

The teacher, obviously shaken by this statement, took little David aside to ask him, "Is that really true about your father?"

"No," said David. "He plays for Glasgow Rangers, but I was too embarrassed to say that in front of the other kids."

* * *

A farmer is helping a cow give birth when he notices his four-year-old son standing wide-eyed at the fence, witnessing the entire thing.

"Dammit," the man says to himself. "Now I'm going to have to explain about the birds and the bees."

Not wanting to jump the gun, the man decides to wait and scc if his son asks any questions.

After everything is finished, he walks over to his lad and asks, "Well, son, do you have any questions?"

"Just one," the child says.

"How fast was the calf going when it hit that cow?"

* * *

A little boy is the subject of a bitter argument between mum and dad in court. Each of them wants him to live with them. The judge notices the boy's distraught face and beckons him to a private audience while he adjourns the court.

"I guess nobody actually thought of asking you what you'd like to do," the judge says to him.

"No, they didn't," the boy replies forlornly.

"You can tell me now. Would you like to be with your mum?"

"Nah, she's mad – she hits me all the time."

"Oh, this wasn't mentioned anywhere in the case," the judge notes with a frown. "So you'd prefer to be with your dad then?"

"Nah, not really. He hits me even worse than my mum does."

The judge is quite appalled by the little boy's situation.

"Well, is there anywhere you'd like to go? I mean, I'm the judge, I can make things happen."

A ray of hope shines on the boy's face. "I'd like to live with Watford Football Club."

"Watford Football Club?" the judge exclaims. "What on earth for?"

"Well, they never beat anyone."

* * *

One night a woman finds her husband standing
over their newborn baby's crib. Silently she watches
him as the bloke's expression reveals disbelief,
delight, amazement, scepticism and enchantment.
Touched by this unusual display of deep emotion,
she slips her arms round her husband. "A penny for
your thoughts," she asks.

"It's amazing," the bloke replies. "I just can't
see how anyone can make a crib like that for only
£46.50."

* * *

A little boy saw a gardener working on his
allotment carrying a huge great bucketful of
steaming dung.

"Phwoa!" said the boy when he caught a sniff of
the whiff. "What are you going to do with that?"
"Aha," said the gardener, "I'm going to put it on my
strawberries."

"Yeeuch!!" yelled the boy. "We have cream on
ours!"

* * *

A little boy is at the post office with his mum one day. They are at the counter to pay for some stationery, when a police officer comes in. He walks to the counter and asks the sales assistant if he can borrow some Sellotape. The clerk hands the sticky tape over and the policeman proceeds to put the picture of a wanted criminal on the wall.

The little boy approaches him and asks, "This is a photo of somebody you're looking for?"

"It is, son. The detectives want him very badly."

"If you want him so badly, why didn't you keep him when you took his picture?" he asks the policeman in a puzzled tone.

* * *

A kindergarten teacher is helping this little boy
to put his boots on. He needs some help and she
soon sees why: they're very tight indeed. After 15
minutes of pushing and pulling, she manages to
fit the boots on the little boy's feet, when he says:
"They're on the wrong feet."

Groaning, the teacher checks – and, indeed, she's
done it wrong. She spends another 15 minutes
taking them off and another 15 putting them back
on the right feet.

"These aren't my boots," the little boy says.
The teacher takes a deep breath, ready to scream
something along the lines of, "Why didn't you say
so before, you moron?" but she bites her tongue
and remains silent. She struggles to take the boots
off and asks where his own boots are.

The little boy points innocently at the pair of
boots she's just taken off and says in a serious tone,
"They're my brother's boots. My mum couldn't
find mine this morning, so she made me wear these
ones."

The teacher is close to tears. With a mighty effort
of will, she refrains from hurling the damn boots

across the room and instead she puts them back on the little boy. It takes a while, but at last he is ready to go out. The teacher is dishevelled and sweaty. Her arms and shoulders ache.

"Right. We're done with the boots. Where are your mittens?"

"I packed them at the bottom of my boots."

* * *

The children had all been photographed, and the teacher was trying to persuade them each to buy a copy of the group picture.

"Just think how nice it will be to look at when you are all grown up and say, 'There's Jennifer; she's a lawyer,' or 'That's Michael; he's a doctor'."

A small voice at the back of the room rang out, "And there's the teacher. She's dead."

* * *

A Sunday school teacher asks her little charges, as they're on the way to the church service: "Why do we have to be quiet in church?"

One bright little girl replies, "Because people are sleeping."

* * *

The boss of a big company needs to call one of his employees about an urgent problem with one of the main computers. He dials the employee's home phone number and is greeted with a child's whispered, "Hello?"

Feeling put out at the inconvenience of having to talk to a youngster, the boss asks, "Is your Daddy home?"

"Yes," whispers the small voice.

"May I talk to him?" the man asks.

To the boss' surprise, the small voice whispers, "No."

Wanting to talk to an adult, the boss asks, "Is your Mummy there?"

"Yes," comes the answer.

"May I talk to her?"

Again the small voice whispers, "No."

Knowing it is unlikely that a young child would be left home alone, the boss decides just to leave a message with the person who should be there watching over the child.

"Is there anyone there besides you?" he asks.

"Yes," whispers the child, "a policeman."

Wondering what on earth a policeman is doing at his employee's house, he says, "And can I talk to this policeman?"

"No, he's busy talking to Mummy and Daddy and the fireman, too."

The boss is growing quite worried when the conversation is drowned out by a deep rumbling sound.

"What was that noise?" he asks the child.

"The search team's helicopter just landed," the small voice whispers back.

"A search team? What for? What are they looking for?" the boss cries, alarmed.

"Me," giggles the little voice.

* * *

At school, the kids are asked to think about hygiene. The teacher has devised a little role play exercise and has asked her pupils to think about what their parents say at the table when they share food.

"My mum always says to go and wash my hands," little Suzy says.

"That's good," the teacher says. "You should always wash your hands before eating, so that you don't get germs and microbes into your food." She looks at the forest of raised hands and picks another pupil.

"My mum always says to me not to play with my food," little Bob says.

"Correct," the teacher congratulates Bob. "If you play with your food, you might drop it or you might not chew correctly."

She notices that little Tim didn't raise his hand. She knows he is a bit shy. Wanting to push him a bit to interact with the rest of the group, she asks him, "What about you, Tim? What do your parents say before you eat?"

"Order something cheap," Tim replies, his eyes downcast.

* * *

It's Christmas, and a man wants to buy a Barbie doll for his daughter. He goes to the toy shop.

"I'd like a Barbie for my daughter," he says to the assistant. "Do you have any?"

"Oh, yes. We have the entire Barbie collection here. Barbie Goes to School for £45, Barbie Goes to Church for £42.50, Barbie and her favourite pony for £75, Pop Star Barbie at £60 and Divorced Barbie at £3,500."

"£3,500? How come this one is much more expensive than the rest?"

"Well, it comes with Ken's house, Ken's car, Ken's furniture and Ken's boat…"

* * *

The teacher asks little Vicky to try to use the word "disappointment" in a sentence. She wants to broaden her pupils' vocabulary and she often gives them quick surprise exercises like this.

Little Vicky is at a loss. She thinks hard for a minute and then she smiles broadly.

"I know! I heard mum say this once, 'I'm sorry, doctor, but the traffic made me late for disappointment.'"

* * *

A man and woman have been married for what seems like forever. They have eight grown-up children and countless grandchildren. On their sixtieth wedding anniversary they have a very candid conversation.

The wife says to her husband, "Honey, since we are so old now, and we've been together for so long, I'm going to be totally honest with you. Is there anything you'd like to know about me and our relationship over the past six decades that you'd like to ask me about? If there is, I promise that I will answer you with total honesty."

The husband pauses for a while, and then says, "Dear, this isn't easy for me to say, but there is actually something that has been eating away at me for quite a few years now. It's just that of all our kids, there's one who looks decidedly different from the others. You know the one I mean, I'm sure, and I'm sure it's nothing but, as I say, I've wondered about this for years, and I would like to know if he had a different father from the rest of the kids."

The wife looks down at her feet and sighs loudly, "Well, dear, I'm sorry to say it, but you're right.

I cannot tell a lie. That child did indeed have a different father from all the others."

The husband looks miserable, but he's still curious. "And who would that be?" he asks.

"Well, dear…" begins the wife slowly, "…you."

* * *

A woman has had a baby. She is very proud of the tiny thing and swears she's going to take care of her and love her.

She goes back home after the delivery, and her husband installs her on the sofa while he goes to check that everything is ready for the new baby. "I'm so proud of you, honey! What a wonderful baby you've given us."

The woman is over the moon and spends the next few days in contentment, until her husband notices a bad smell in the cot. He leans forward and feels about and realises in horror that the baby is covered in poo.

"Honey, what's happened? Didn't you change the baby's nappy?"

"It's all right, darling. I checked! It says on the box: 'Suitable for up to twenty pounds.'"

* * *

A policeman is walking down the street, when he spots a woman with the front of her blouse open and one of her breasts hanging out.

He goes up to her and says, "Lady, I could book you for indecent exposure! Please cover yourself!"

The woman looks at him uncomprehendingly and then looks down.

"Oh my God!" she exclaims. "I left the baby on the bus!"

* * *

The phone at the local hospital rings, and the duty medic picks it up to hear a man jabbering on the other end.

"My wife's contractions are only two minutes apart!" he says.

"Is this her first child?" the doctor asks.

"No, you idiot," the man shouts, "This is her husband!"

DEATH

A man placed some flowers on the grave of his mother and was starting back towards his car when his attention was diverted to another man kneeling at a grave. The man kept repeating, "Why did you have to die?"

The first man approached him and said, "I don't wish to interfere with your private grief, but can I ask who you're mourning for?"

The mourner took a moment to collect himself, then replied, "My wife's first husband."

* * *

Two men waiting at the Pearly Gates strike up a conversation.

"How'd you die?" the first man asks the second.

"I froze to death," says the second.

"That's awful," says the first man. "How does it feel to freeze to death?"

"It's very uncomfortable at first," says the second man. "You get the shakes, and you get pains in all your fingers and toes. But eventually, it's a very calm way to go. You get numb and you kind of drift off, as if you're sleeping. How about you, how did you die?"

"I had a heart attack," says the first man. "You see, I knew my wife was cheating on me, so one day I showed up at home unexpectedly. I ran up to the bedroom, and found her alone, knitting. I ran down to the basement, but no one was hiding there. I ran up to the second floor, but no one was hiding there either. I ran as fast as I could to the attic, and just as I got there, I had a massive heart attack and died."

The second man shakes his head. "That's so ironic," he says.

"What do you mean?" asks the first man.

"If you'd only stopped to look in the freezer, we'd both still be alive."

* * *

On their way to get married, a young couple are involved in a fatal car accident. The couple find themselves sitting outside the Pearly Gates waiting for St Peter to process them into heaven. While waiting, they begin to wonder; could they possibly get married in heaven? When St Peter shows up, they ask him.

St Peter says, "I don't know. This is the first time anyone has asked. Let me go and find out."

He goes off to get to the bottom of it. The couple sit down to wait for an answer... for a couple of months. St Peter finally returns looking somewhat bedraggled.

"Yes," he informs the couple, "you can get married in heaven."

"Great!" says the couple. "But we were just wondering, what if things don't work out? Could we also get a divorce in heaven?"

St Peter, red-faced with anger, slams his clipboard on to the ground.

"What's wrong?" ask the frightened couple.

"Come on!" St Peter shouts. "It took me three months to find a priest up here! Do you have any idea how long it'll take me to find a lawyer?"

* * *

Two men are scheduled to die in the electric chair on the same day. The chaplain and the director of the prison will assist the proceedings. Before they give the go-ahead for the execution however, they have to perform one last rite: granting the last request of the condemned.

The chaplain approaches the first prisoner and asks him, "My son, do you have a last request?"

"Yeah, I do," he replies. "I'm very fond of music. I'd like to hear a song one last time, the song that was playing on the jukebox when I met my wife. Could you play 'Candle in the Wind' by Elton John for me one last time?"

The chaplain glances sideways at the director of the prison, who nods his agreement.

"Very well," the father says. "You will hear this song once more before the execution. What about you, my son?" he asks the other guy. "Do you have a last request?"

"Yeah," the prisoner says with a grimace. "Could you do me first?"

* * *

Three women die together in an accident and go to heaven.

When they get there, St Peter says, "We only have

one rule here in heaven: don't step on the ducks."

Sure enough, there are ducks everywhere in heaven. It is almost impossible not to step on a duck and, although they try their best to avoid them, the first woman accidentally steps on one. Along comes St Peter with the ugliest man she ever saw.

St Peter chains them together and says, "Your punishment for stepping on a duck is to spend eternity chained to this ugly man."

The next day, the second woman steps on a duck and along comes St Peter. With him is another extremely ugly man.

He chains them together with the same admonition as he gave the first woman.

The third woman, having observed all this, is very, very careful where she steps. She manages to go months without stepping on any ducks, but one day St Peter comes up to her with the most handsome man she's ever seen and, silently, he chains them together. The happy woman says, "Wonder what I did to deserve being chained to you for all of eternity?"

The guy says, "I don't know about you, but I stepped on a duck."

A murderer, sitting in the
electric chair, is about
to be executed.

"Have you any last
requests?" asks the chaplain.

"Yes," replies the murderer.
"Will you hold my hand?"

* * *

Two men were asked what they would like
to be said about them at their funerals.

The first one says, "I want someone to say
I was the greatest footballer ever."

The other man says, "I want someone to
say, 'He's moving, he's moving!'"

* * *

A Manchester United fan dies one match day and
goes to heaven in his Manchester United shirt.
Arriving at the top of the ethereal staircase, he
knocks on the pearly gates, and out walks St Peter

with a Manchester City scarf round his neck.

"I'm sorry mate," says St Peter. "No Manchester United fans in heaven."

"What?" exclaims the man, astonished.

"You heard, no Manchester United fans."

"But, but… I've been a good man," replies the Manchester United supporter.

"Oh really," says St Peter, "what have you done then?"

"Well," says the guy, "a month before I died, I gave £10 to starving children in Africa."

"Oh," says St Peter, "anything else?"

"Well, two weeks before I died I also gave £10 to the homeless."

"Hmmm. Anything else?"

"Yeah, on the way home yesterday, I gave £10 to the Albanian orphans."

"Okay," says St Peter. "You wait here a moment while I have a word with the boss."

Ten minutes pass, St Peter returns and looks the fan straight in the eye. "I've had a word with God and he agrees with me," he says. "Here's your £30 back – now get lost!"

* * *

Three men are walking through the jungle, when a native tribe ambushes them. The leader of the tribe offers each man one last request before being killed for trespassing. The first man asks for a big feast, so the tribe give him their best food and when he's full, they chop off his head.

"We shall make him into a canoe!" the leader exclaims.

The next man pleads to have sex one last time, so the tribe gets their sexiest woman and he has the best sex of his life.

Then the tribe chop off his head and again the leader says, "We shall make him into a canoe!"

The last man thinks for a second, then requests a fork. The tribe look confused, but give him a fork a.

Then the man starts to stab himself all over and shouts, "You're not making a bloody canoe out of me!"

* * *

A man was leaving a cafe with his morning coffee, when he noticed a most unusual funeral procession approaching the cemetery. A long black hearse was followed by a second hearse. Behind the second hearse was a solitary man walking a pit bull on a leash. Behind him was a queue of 200 men walking in single file.

The man couldn't stand the curiosity, so he respectfully approached the man walking the dog. "I am so sorry for your loss, and I know now is a bad time to disturb you, but I've never seen a funeral like this with so many people walking in single file. Whose funeral is it?"

The man replied, "Well that first hearse is for my wife."

"What happened to her?"

"My dog attacked and killed her."

He enquired further. "Well, who is in the second hearse then?"

"The mother-in-law. She tried to save my wife and, lo and behold, the dog turned on her and killed her as well."

A poignant moment of silence passed between the men. "Can I borrow the dog?"

"Yeah, of course you can mate, but you'll have to join the queue!"

* * *

A woman sent flowers to someone who was moving to Spain for a job promotion. She also sent flowers the same day to a funeral for a friend. Later, she found that the flower shop had got the cards mixed up.

The man who was moving received the card that said, "Deepest condolences," and the card they sent to the funeral home said, "I know it's hot where you're going, but you deserve it."

* * *

Brenda is at home making dinner, when her husband's work mate Bill arrives at her door.

"Brenda, can I come in?" he asks. "I've something to tell you."

"Of course you can come in. But where's my husband?" enquires Brenda.

"That's what I'm here to tell you, Brenda. There was an accident down at the Guinness brewery."

"Oh, God, no!" cries Brenda. "Please don't tell me."

"I must, Brenda. Your husband is dead and gone. I'm sorry."

Finally, she looks up at Bill. "How did it happen?"

"It was terrible, Brenda. He fell into a vat of Guinness and drowned."

"Oh, my dear Jesus! Did he at least go quickly?" sobbed Brenda.

"Well, no, Brenda. Fact is, he got out three times to pee."

* * *

A funeral service is being held for a woman who has recently died. Right at the end of the service, the bearers pick up the coffin and begin to carry it to where it will enter the cremation chamber and be burned. As they turn a corner in the chapel, the coffin hits the wall and there is a loud, audible "OUCH!" from inside it. They drop the casket to the floor, and it turns out that, wonder of all wonders, the woman is actually alive. The woman lives for two more years and then dies – for real this time. Everyone goes through the same ceremony, but this time, as the bearers round the corner, the woman's husband shouts out, "Careful, you lot. Watch out for the wall!"

A man was passing through a small
town when he came upon a huge funeral
procession.
"Who died?" he asked a nearby local.
"I'm not sure," replied the local, "but I
think it's the one in the coffin."

* * *

In the middle of poker night, John loses a £500
hand, clutches his chest, and drops dead on the
floor. His mate Pete is designated as the guy who
has to go and give his wife the bad news.

"Be gentle with her, Pete," one of the other
players says. "They were childhood sweethearts."

So Pete walks over to John's house, knocks on the
door, and tries his best to be helpful. "Your husband
just lost £500 playing cards."

"Tell that idiot to drop dead," shouts
the wife.

"I'll tell him," Pete says.

* * *

A man is standing at the Pearly Gates before St Peter.

"All you need to have done is one good deed, and we will allow you passage into heaven."

The man says, "No problem. I was stopped at a crossroads once and saw a gang of blokes harassing a young woman. I got out of my car, walked up to the leader, who was over seven feet tall and must have weighed nearly 15 stone, and I told him that abusing a woman is a cowardly act, and that I would not tolerate it. I then reached up, yanked out his nose ring and kicked him in the balls to make a point."

St Peter is amazed and starts searching the man's life in his book in front of him and says, "I can't find that incident anywhere in your file. When did that happen?"

The man looks down at his watch and says, "Oh, about two minutes ago."

* * *

Three Aussies were working on a high-rise building project – Steve, Bruce and Bluey. Steve falls off and is killed instantly.

As the ambulance takes the body away, Bruce says, "Someone should go and tell his wife."

Bluey says, "OK. I'm pretty good at that sensitive stuff, so let me do it." Two hours later, he comes back carrying a crate of beer.

Bruce says, "Where did you get that from, Bluey?"

"Steve's wife gave it to me," Bluey replies.

"That's unbelievable," says Bruce. "You told the lady her husband was dead and she gave you the beer?"

"Well, not exactly," Bluey says. "When she answered the door, I said to her, 'You must be Steve's widow.' She said, 'I'm not a widow.' And I said, 'I'll bet you a crate of beer you are'."

DISASTERS, ACCIDENTS AND INJURIES

A shop window had been smashed by a falling tree in a storm. The shop owner called in a specialist company to remove the old broken window and install a new one. The shopkeeper watched as one workman hacked the broken pieces out of the window frame. The workman stuck his head in through the broken window.

"Any chance of a cup of tea?" he called.

Just then a large piece of glass fell from the top of the window frame and chopped off the workman's ear.

"AAARRGH!" screamed the workman. "That glass just chopped off me ear!"

The shopkeeper spotted an ear lying on the floor. "Is this it?" he asked, anxious to help.

"Naw," said the workman. "Mine had a pencil behind it!"

* * *

A photographer for a national magazine is assigned to get photos of a great forest fire. Smoke at the scene is too thick to get any good shots, so he frantically calls his office to hire a plane.

"It will be waiting for you at the airport!" he is assured by his editor.

As soon as he gets to the small, rural airport, sure enough, a plane is warming up near the runway. He jumps in with his equipment and yells, "Let's go! Let's go!" The pilot swings the plane into the wind and soon they are airborne.

"Fly over the north side of the fire," says the photographer, "and make three or four low-level passes."

"Why?" asks the pilot.

"Because I'm going to take pictures! I'm a photographer, and photographers take pictures!" says the photographer with great exasperation.

After a long gulp, the pilot says, "You mean you're not the instructor?"

A couple have a car crash. They are both OK, except that the wife ends up with a nasty scar on her cheek. The only thing doctors can suggest is plastic surgery.

Unfortunately, there are few places on the body that match the smoothness and grain of the face. One of these places is the buttocks but, understandably, the woman is rather reluctant to have any skin removed from her bottom to be grafted on to her face; she doesn't really want to have a scarred bottom any more than she is prepared to accept a scarred face.

"Don't worry, honey," her husband says. "I'll donate some skin from my bum. I don't mind, I wouldn't like you to have a scarred bottom either. I love your bottom as it is too much for that."

The wife is ecstatic, and can't believe that her husband will sacrifice his body for her.

The operation goes ahead as planned and, after a few weeks, the wife's face is once again smooth and beautiful.

A year passes, and they go out to celebrate the day they survived the terrible accident.

"Darling, I'm so proud of you. I don't know what to do to repay you for what you did for me," she says over a glass of wine in a fancy restaurant.

"It's OK, honey. I get all the reward I need every time your mother kisses you on the cheeks."

* * *

A fire starts inside a chemical plant and the alarm goes out to fire stations miles around. After crews have been fighting the fire for more than an hour, the chemical company president approaches the fire chief and says, "All our secret formulae are in the vault. They must be saved. I'll give £100,000 to the firemen who bring them out safely."

Suddenly, another engine comes roaring down the road and drives straight into the middle of the inferno. The other men watch, unbelieving, as the firemen hop off their engine and heroically extinguish the fire, saving the secret formulae. The company president walks over to reward the volunteers and asks them, "What do you fellers plan to do with the money?"

The driver looks him right in the eye and answers, "Well, the first thing we're going to do is fix the brakes."

* * *

Cruising at 40,000 feet, an airplane suddenly shudders and a passenger looks out of the window. "Sh*t!" he screams, "one of the engines just blew up!"

Other passengers leave their seats and come running over. Suddenly, the aircraft is rocked by a second blast as yet another engine explodes on the other side.

The passengers are in a panic now and even the stewardesses can't maintain order. Just then, standing tall and smiling confidently, the pilot strides from the cockpit and assures everyone that there is nothing to worry about. His words and his demeanour make most of the passengers feel better, so they sit down as the pilot calmly walks to the door of the aircraft.

There, he grabs several packages from under the seats and hands them to the flight attendants. Each crew member attaches the package to their backs.

"Say," says an alert passenger, "aren't those parachutes?"

The pilot nods with a smile. The passenger goes on, "But I thought you said there was nothing to worry about?"

"There isn't," replies the pilot as a third engine explodes.

"We're just going to get help."

* * *

While flying to South Africa, a plane crashes in desolate mountain terrain. The only survivor is an elderly lady who manages to stumble out of the wreckage. After crawling, hungry and exhausted, for several miles she finds shelter in a cave. After some time, a Red Cross search party arrives and begins crossing the mountain range looking for survivors. After a few hours, they spot the cave entrance.

"Is anyone alive in there?" shouts the group leader.

"Who's that?" shouts the old lady.

"Red Cross!" answers the leader.

"Jesus, you guys get everywhere!" shouts the old dear. "I've already donated."

* * *

It was a tough rugby match. One player left the pitch with a broken nose, a fat lip, a torn ear, two broken teeth and a mangled finger, but he hadn't a clue who they belonged to.

* * *

During an interview for a points operator on the railway, the chief engineer asks a job candidate, "What would you do if the Plymouth-to-London was heading north on track one and the London-to-Plymouth was heading south on track one?"

"I'd definitely call my brother," the interviewee replies.

"Why on earth would you call your brother?" the chief engineer asks.

"Because he's never seen a train crash before," the applicant replies.

DOCTORS

A mechanic was removing the cylinder head from the engine of a Jaguar, when he spotted a well-known heart surgeon in his garage, waiting for the service manager to look at his car.

The mechanic shouted across the garage, "Hey, Doc. Could I ask you a question?"

The surgeon, a bit surprised, walked over to the mechanic. The mechanic straightened up, wiped his hands on a rag and asked, "So, Doc, take a look at this engine. I open its heart, take valves out, fix 'em, put 'em back in, and when I finish, it works just like new. So how come I get such a small salary, and you get loads of money when you and I are doing basically the same work?"

The surgeon paused, smiled and leaned over, and then whispered to the mechanic, "Try doing it with the engine running."

While making his rounds, a doctor points out an X-ray to a group of medical students.

"As you can see," he begins, "the patient has a limp because his left fibula and tibia are radically arched."

The doctor turns to one of the students and asks, "What would you do in a case like this?"

"Well," ponders the student, "I suppose I'd limp, too."

* * *

A man goes to the doctor and tells him that he's really worried because every part of his body hurts.

"Show me where," says the doctor, concerned.

The man touches his own arm and screams, "Ouch!" He touches his leg, his nose, his elbow and every time he howls in pain.

He looks at the doctor and says, "See? I told you. It hurts everywhere!'

The doctor pokes him in the chest and says, 'No. Don't worry, it's not serious. You've just got a broken index finger.'

A bunch of first-year medical students were receiving their first anatomy class with a real dead human body. They all gathered around the surgery table with the body covered with a white sheet. The professor started the class by telling them, "It is absolutely necessary to have two important qualities as a Doctor of Medicine. The first has to be that you're not disgusted by anything involving the human body."

As an example, the professor pulled back the sheet, rolled the body over and stuck his finger up the corpse's rectum, withdrew it, and then stuck it in his mouth.

"Go ahead and do the same thing," he told his students.

The students freaked out, hesitated for several minutes, but eventually took turns sticking a finger up the dead body's rectum and then sucking on it.

When everyone had finished, and they were all looking queasy, the professor looked at them and said, "The second most important quality is observation. I inserted my middle finger and sucked on my index finger. Now learn to pay attention!"

* * *

An attractive young girl, chaperoned by an ugly old lady, enters a doctor's office.

"We've come for an examination," says the young girl.

"All right," says the doctor. "Go behind that curtain and take your clothes off."

"No, not me," says the girl, "it's my old aunt here."

"Very well," says the doctor. "Madam, stick out your tongue."

* * *

After surgery, a man wakes up drowsily in the hospital.

He yells to the nurse, "I can't feel my legs!"

"Well, of course you can't," she replies. "You have just had your arms amputated."

* * *

A man visits his GP with a delicate matter. "I was thinking about getting a vasectomy."

"Well, that's a big decision," says the doctor. "Have you talked it over with your family?"

"Oh, yes," says the man. "They're in favour of it, 15 to 7."

* * *

With a screech of brakes, an ambulance pulls up at the local casualty ward and a hippie is wheeled out on a hospital trolley.

The doctor questions the man's hippie friends about his situation.

"So what was he doing then?" asks the physician. "Acid?

Cannabis?"

"Sort of," replies one of the hippies, nervously thumbing his kaftan, "but we ran out of gear, so I skinned up a home-made spliff."

"And what was in that?" asks the doctor.

"Um… I kind of raided my girlfriend's spice rack," says the hippie. "There was a bit of cumin, some turmeric and a little paprika."

"Well, that explains it," the doctor replies, looking at them gravely. "He's in a korma."

* * *

A doctor says to his patient, "I have bad news and worse news."

"Oh, dear. What's the bad news?" asks the patient.

The doctor replies, "You only have 24 hours to live."

"That's terrible," says the patient. "How can the other news possibly be worse?"

The doctor replies, "I've been trying to contact you since yesterday."

* * *

A doctor walks into a bank. Preparing to sign a cheque, he accidentally pulls a rectal thermometer out of his shirt pocket and tries to write with it. Realising his mistake, he looks at the thermometer with annoyance and says, "Well, that's just great. Some asshole's got my pen!"

DRINKING

A guy walks into a bar and orders a double whisky – straight. As he begins to drink he reaches into his wallet and pulls out a photograph. He takes a quick peek at it and then puts it back in his wallet quickly. He then finishes his whisky, calls the barkeep over and orders another. He begins to drink it and, as he does so, he reaches into his wallet and pulls out the photograph again, looks at it and then puts it away quickly. He continues doing this for about an hour.

Eventually the barkeep asks him, "Hey, mate, what's with the photo? I'm not worried by the amount you're drinking, I'd just really like to have a look at the pic – what on earth is it?"

The man replies, "It's a photograph of my wife. When she starts to look good, I know it's time to go home!"

* * *

Four men are sitting in a bar, when a guy comes up to them and offers them a bet. He reckons that he can place a pint glass on the bar, twenty-five feet away, and he can stand behind their table and piss right into – and fill – the pint glass. The men all confer and decide that there's no way this guy can do it. They quickly stump up the hundred quid that he's offering. The man walks to the bar, places an empty pint glass on it and returns to where the men are. He stands there, drops his trousers and begins to piss. It goes everywhere apart from the pint glass – he doesn't even get close to it and even pisses on the men with whom he's made the bet. They can't help laughing at his piss-poor effort. When the guy has finished, he hands over the hundred quid.

One of the men turns and asks him, "What the hell made you think you could fill that glass all the way over there?"

"I never thought I could," said the guy, "but I bet the bartender five hundred quid that I could piss all over you blokes and you'd just laugh about it!"

* * *

A man is sitting in a rough bar, drinking. He orders a fresh pint but suddenly is overcome with the urge to go to the toilet. He doesn't trust anyone in the crummy bar but he has to go, so he scribbles on a cigarette paper, "I spat in this. Don't drink it!" and he gums the paper to the side of his pint glass. He goes off to the toilet and comes back a couple of minutes later to find another cigarette paper stuck to his glass.

On it is written, "So did we!"

* * *

Proudly showing off his new apartment to some friends late one night, a drunk leads the way to his bedroom. When they get there, they see that there's a big brass gong taking pride of place.

"What's with that gong?" one of the friends asks.

"That's no gong," the drunk replies. "It's a talking clock!"

"Oh yeah? How does it work, then?" the friend asks.

"Watch," the drunk says. He moves to the corner of the room, picks up a hammer and pounds the gong as loudly as he can.

Suddenly, someone on the other side of the wall starts screaming, "What the hell do you think you're doing? It's three o'clock in the bloody morning!"

* * *

A drunken man gets on the bus late one night outside the pub, staggers up the aisle and sits next to an elderly woman.

She looks the man up and down and says in a very reproving tone, "I've got news for you. You're going straight to hell!"

"Man, I'm on the wrong bus!" shouts the man, jumping up out of his seat.

* * *

Mike staggers home very late after another late-night drinking session with his best mates and removes his shoes to avoid waking his missus. He tiptoes as quietly as he can towards the stairs but trips and knocks a vase on to the floor, which he then falls on to, cutting his buttocks. Managing not to shout, he stands up and pulls his pants down to examine the damage in the hall mirror. His backside is cut and bleeding, so he grabs a box of plasters and sticks them wherever he can see blood. He then hides the almost empty plaster box and stumbles into bed.

The next morning, Mike awakes with searing pain in both his head and his bum, to see his wife staring at him.

"You were drunk again last night, weren't you?" she says.

"Why would you say such a mean thing?" he asks.

"Well," she says, "it could be the open front door. Or the broken glass at the bottom of the stairs. Or the drops of blood on the stairs. It could even be your bloodshot eyes. But mostly, it's all those bloody plasters stuck to the hall mirror!"

* * *

Dave and Jim worked as aeroplane mechanics in London. One day, the airport was fogbound and they were stuck in the hangar.

Dave said, "I wish we had a drink."

"Me, too," replied Jim. "Y'know, I've heard you can drink jet fuel and get a buzz. You want to try it?"

So they poured themselves a couple of glasses and got completely smashed.

The next morning, Dave woke up and was surprised at how good he felt. Then the phone rang and it was Jim.

"Hey, how do you feel this morning?" he asked.

"I feel great," said Dave. "How about you?"

"I feel great, too." Jim responded.

"Have you broken wind yet?"

"No," said Dave.

"Well, don't – I'm in Glasgow!"

* * *

An armless man walks into a bar, which is empty except for the bartender. He orders a pint of Guinness and, when he is served, asks the bartender if he would get the money from his wallet in his pocket, since he has no arms.

The bartender obliges him. He then asks if the bartender would tip the glass to his lips. The bartender does this until the man finishes his pint. He then asks if the bartender could get a hanky from his pocket and wipe the foam from his lips. The bartender does this and comments that it must be very difficult not to have any arms and have to ask someone to do nearly everything for him.

The man says, "Yes, it is a bit embarrassing at times. By the way, where's your restroom?"

The bartender quickly replies, "The closest one is in the petrol station down the street."

* * *

Four fonts walk into a bar. Barman says, "Oi! Get out! We don't want your type in here!"

* * *

A drunk man is walking down the street, his hands to his bloody nose. A cop can't help noticing he seems to have taken a beating.

"Can you describe the person who did this to you, sir?" he asks.

"That's exactly what I was doing when this guy hit me, officer," he replies.

* * *

A man walks into a pub with a neck brace, orders a pint and asks the landlord, "Who's in the lounge?"

The landlord replies, "There's 15 people playing darts."

The man says, "Get them a pint, too." Then he asks, "Who's upstairs?"

The landlord replies, "150 people at the disco."

The man says, "Get them pints, too."

"That'll be £1,095, please," says the landlord.

The man replies, "Sorry, I haven't got that much money on me."

The landlord remarks, "If you were at the pub down the road, they'd have broken your neck."

"Just been there," says the man.

* * *

A man walks into a pub, sits down, orders three pints of lager, drinks them and then leaves. This continues daily for several weeks.

Curious, the pub landlord approaches him one day. "Why do you always order three pints of lager?" he asks.

"Well," says the man, "my two brothers and I always used to have a pint each and since they've both passed on, I've continued to order the three beers in their honour."

The landlord is taken aback by such nobility and welcomes the man whenever he then visits the pub. But two weeks later, the man strolls in and orders not his usual three pints, but only two. Surprised, the landlord asks what the problem is.

"Oh, no problem at all," smiles the man. "I've just decided to stop drinking."

* * *

After a few beers, a guy has to head for the gents'. He sits down and starts his business when he hears another person entering the cubicle next to him.

Then he hears, "How are you doing?"

The guy is quite shocked and doesn't know what to say. Finally, he says, "Er… I'm fine, thanks."

"You're having a good time?"

The guy is embarrassed; he's never found himself in such a situation before. "Er… yeah, it's all right."

There is a short silence, then the voice is heard again. "Listen, I'll call you back in a moment.

There's an idiot in the next cubicle who keeps talking to me."

* * *

Every night after dinner, Harry was in the habit of heading off to the local tavern. He would spend the whole evening there and would come back home very drunk around midnight every night.

His wife, waiting up for him, would go to the door and let him in. Then she would proceed to yell and scream at him, for his constant nights out, his coming home in a drunken state, for longer and longer every year – but Harry carried on.

One day, the wife cracked and sought counsel from one of her friends. The friend listened to her patiently and then said, "Why don't you treat him a little differently when he comes home? Instead of shouting at him, why don't you welcome him home with some kind words and a kiss? That might make him change his ways." The wife thought it over and convinced herself that might be a good idea. In any case, it wouldn't hurt to try.

So that night, after dinner, Harry took off again. About midnight, he arrived home in his usual condition. His wife heard him at the door and let Harry in. This time, instead of shouting at him, as she had always done, she took his arm and led him into the living room. She sat him down in an easy chair, put his feet up on a stool and took his shoes off. Then she went behind him and started to cuddle him a little and massage his shoulders.

After a little while, she said to him, "It's pretty late, dear. What about going upstairs to bed now?"

At that, Harry replied, in his inebriated state, "I guess we might as well. I'll be getting into trouble with the stupid wife when I get home anyway!"

* * *

A pony walks into a bar and says, "May I have a drink?"

The barman frowns and says, "What? I can't hear you. Speak up!"

"May I please have a drink?"

"What? You'll have to speak up!"

"Could I please have a drink?"

"Now, listen. If you don't speak up, I won't serve you."

"I'm sorry. I'm just a little hoarse."

* * *

A man walks in through the front door of a bar.
He is obviously drunk. He staggers up to the bar,
seats himself on a stool and, with a belch, asks
the bartender for a drink. The bartender politely
informs the man that it appears he has already
had plenty to drink. Consequently, he will not be
serving him any more drinks, but he could call him
a cab.

The drunk is briefly surprised, then softly scoffs,
grumbles, climbs down off the barstool and staggers
out the front door.

A few minutes later, the same drunk stumbles
in the side door of the bar. He wobbles up to the
bar and hollers for a drink. The bartender comes
over and, still politely – although a bit more firmly
– refuses service to the man due to his inebriation.
Again, the bartender offers to call a cab for him.

The drunk looks at the bartender for a moment
angrily, curses and shows himself out via the side
door, all the while grumbling and shaking his head.

A few minutes later, the same drunk bursts in
through the back door of the bar. He plops himself

up on a bar stool, gathers his wits and belligerently orders a drink.

The bartender comes over and emphatically reminds the man that he is clearly drunk, will be served no drinks and that either a cab or the police will be called immediately.

The surprised drunk looks at the bartender and in hopeless anguish cries, "Man! How many bars do you work at?"

* * *

One night, a drunk comes stumbling into a bar and says to the bartender, "Drinks for everyone on me, including you, bartender."

So the bartender follows the guy's orders and when all the drinks have been handed over says, "That'll be £150, please."

The drunk admits he has no money. The bartender, incensed, slaps him around and throws him out.

The next night the same drunk comes in again and orders a drink for everyone in the bar, including the bartender.

Again the bartender follows his instructions, and once again the drunk says he has no money. The bartender slaps him around a bit harder and throws him out once more.

On the third night, the drunk comes in once again and orders drinks for all except the bartender.

"What, no drink for me?" replies the bartender with heavy sarcasm.

"Oh, no. You get violent when you drink."

* * *

A drunk goes to the doctor complaining of tiredness and headaches. "I feel tired all the time," he slurs. "My head hurts and I'm not sleeping. What is it, Doc?"

Frowning, the doctor examines him before standing back. "I can't find anything wrong," he says. "It must be the drinking."

"Fair enough," replies the lush. "I'll come back when you sober up."

* * *

One day, a mechanic was working under a car when some brake fluid accidentally dripped into his mouth. "Wow," said the mechanic to himself. "That stuff tastes good." The following day, he told his mate about his discovery.

"It tastes great," said the mechanic. "I think I'll try a little more today."

The next day, the mechanic told his mate he'd drunk a pint of the stuff. His friend was worried but didn't say anything until the next day, when the mechanic revealed he'd drunk two pints.

"Don't you know that brake fluid is toxic? It's really bad for you," said his mate.

"I know what I'm doing," snapped the mechanic. "I can stop any time I want to."

* * *

A man is in the habit of having a shot of whisky every night before he goes to bed. For years, this habit has been irritating his wife no end, but she's never managed to persuade him to stop.

Fed-up, she decides to resort to a little object lesson one night. She takes two glasses and fills one up with water, the other with whisky. She then opens his tackle box and picks up a worm.

"Look closely," she says to her husband and drops the worm in the glass full of water. The worm wriggles a bit, looking bored, but survives. She then repeats the experiment with another worm, which she drops into the glass full of whisky. The worm thrashes a bit, convulses, then dies.

"See?" she asks triumphantly. "Do you understand what will happen if you keep drinking whisky?"

The husband, without missing a beat, replies cheerfully, "Yes, I see now. If I keep on drinking whisky, I won't get worms!"

* * *

A man walks into a bar after a long day at work. As he begins relaxing and drinking his beer, he hears a seductive voice purr, "You've got great hair!"

He looks around but can't see where the voice is coming from, so he goes back to his beer. A minute or so later, he hears the same soft voice again, which says, "You're a handsome man!" Puzzled, the guy looks around, but still can't see where the voice is coming from. He goes back to his beer, only to hear the voice say, "Like your shirt!"

The man is so baffled by this that he finally goes up to the barman and asks him what is going on.

"Oh, it's nothing," the barman answered. "It's the nuts. They're complimentary."

* * *

A baby boy is born with no arms, no legs and no body, but his father still loves him. Eighteen years pass, and the father takes his son to the pub for his first pint. The son takes his first sip and immediately he grows a torso, so the father tells him to drink again. The son takes another sip and grows some arms and legs. He's so happy, he goes running into the street shouting and waving his arms around, when he's suddenly hit by a lorry. The barman shakes his head sadly. "He should have quit while he was ahead."

* * *

A man walks into a bar and orders a pint of beer. He looks around, admiring the room and the decoration, and he soon notices that there are big lumps of what looks like meat hanging from the ceiling.

"Er… why have you got all this meat hanging down in your bar?" he asks the barman.

"It's a little bet we're running," the barman replies. "If you can jump up and grab a bit of meat in your mouth, then you get all your drinks bought for you. If you fail, then you have to buy a drink for everyone else in the bar. Want to give it a go?"

The man looks at the crowd in the pub and shakes his head. "No," he replies, "the steaks are too high."

* * *

A guy is getting bored alone in a bar after a few beers, so he tries his luck with the girl sitting next to him.

"Do you mind if I ask you a personal question?" he says to her, convinced, in his drunken state, that this is a great chat-up line.

"I don't know," replies the young woman, suspicious. "It depends how personal it is."

"Tell me, how many men have you slept with?"

"I'm not going to tell you that!" the woman exclaimed. "That's my business!"

"Sorry," blurts the guy, with a wave of his hand. "I didn't realise you made a living out of it."

* * *

A man walks into a bar grinning his face off. "The beers are on me!" he says, happily. "My wife has just run off with my best friend."

"That's a shame," says the barman. "Why aren't you sad?"

"Sad?" asks the man. "They've saved me a fortune. They were both pregnant."

* * *

A cowboy is at the bar with a friend.

"You see that guy there at that table, the one with big boots?"

"Er… they all wear big boots."

"The one who's smoking."

'Man, they're all smoking."

"The guy there, the one who's playing poker!"

"Well, they're all playing cards."

Exasperated, the cowboy takes his gun out and shoots three of the four guys at the table.

"Now do you see the one I mean?"

"Yeah, now I do"

"I hate that guy."

* * *

A guy enters a bar and sits down in silence. The bartender sees him and asks, "What'll you have?"

"A scotch, please."

The bartender hands him the drink and says, "That'll be £3."

"What are you talking about? I don't owe you anything for this," the customer replies with a thin smile.

A lawyer, sitting nearby and overhearing the conversation, says to the bartender, "You know, he's got you there. In the original offer, which constitutes a binding contract upon acceptance, there was no stipulation of remuneration."

The bartender is not impressed at all. "OK, you beat me for a drink. But don't ever let me catch you in here again," he says in a grumpy tone and walks off to serve another customer.

The next day, the same guy walks into the bar.

"What the hell are you doing in here? I can't believe you've got the audacity to come back!"

The guy says, "What are you talking about? I've never been here in my life!"

The bartender scratches his head and replies, "I'm very sorry, but this is uncanny. You must have a double."

"Thank you very much, my good man. Make it a scotch," the guy replies with a smile.

* * *

A bloke's in the pub and decides he'd better go, hoping he can manage to get home early enough not to piss off his wife for drinking after work. When he gets home, though, he finds her in bed with his boss. Later, back in the pub, he tells the barman what's just happened.

"That's awful," says the barman. "What did you do?"

"Well, I carefully sneaked back out the door and came back here. I mean, they were only just starting, so I figured I'd got time for a couple more pints!"

* * *

A man and his wife are dining at a table in a plush restaurant, and the husband keeps staring at a drunken lady swigging her drink as she sits alone at a nearby table.

The wife asks, "Do you know her?"

"Yes." sighs the husband, "She's my ex-girlfriend. I understand she took to drinking right after we split up seven years ago, and I hear she hasn't been sober since."

"My God!" says the wife. "Who would think a person could go on celebrating that long?"

DRIVING

A man has just parked his car. He opens up the door to get out and another car speeding by rips the door clean off.

"What?!" the guy wails. "Look at that! My BMW! It's wrecked!"

A passer-by who has witnessed the scene runs to him and says, "Forget about the door! This car's taken your arm as well. We need to take you to hospital as fast as we can."

The guy looks down at his left arm in disbelief. It's gone.

"Oh, no!" he wails. "My Rolex!"

* * *

Headline: A hole has appeared in one of the walls of the ladies' changing rooms at the sports club. Police are looking into it.

* * *

A cop catches a guy speeding, so he flashes his lights and the guy pulls over. The cop looks him over, sniffs and asks, "Sir, have you been drinking? Your eyes are bloodshot."

"So what?" the guy replies. "Your eyes are glazed, have you been eating doughnuts?"

* * *

"I did stop, officer, honest," a driver explains for the fourth time to the officer who's just pulled him over for going through a stop sign.

"You didn't stop, sir," the policeman explains to him for the fourth time. "I was driving right behind you. You did slow down, but you didn't stop."

"Slowing down or stopping, what's the difference?"

At the end of his tether, the policeman grabs his truncheon and proceeds to beat the shit out of the obtuse driver.

"Now," he asks. "Would you like me to stop, or just slow down a little?"

* * *

A young police officer stops a guy who's been speeding.

He asks him to get out and the guy complies.

"All right," the officer says. "May I see your licence, please?"

"I don't have it any more," the driver replies. "You lot took it away last month when I was caught drink-driving."

"Oh, that's lovely," the cop says with heavy sarcasm. "Drink-driving and now speeding with no licence. You have the papers for this car?"

"Dunno. They might be there somewhere, I didn't check when I stole it, I didn't see it in the glove box when I put my gun in there, though."

"You have a gun in the glove box?" the cop asks nervously.

"I guess I could have left it with the dead guy in the boot, but you never know when this kind of thing might come in handy."

"There's a corpse in the boot?" the policeman backs up, takes his gun out and feels for his radio through the open window. He keeps the driver under the barrel of the gun until more patrol cars turn up.

His colleagues take him to the side, and the sergeant interrogates the driver.

"I'll need your licence number, if you can remember it."

Wordlessly, the guy hands out his driving licence. He follows this with the car's papers.

"Everything seems to be in order," the sergeant says, squinting at the licence and ownership papers. He casts a glance at the policeman who's made the call and is now talking, wild-eyed, to the other policemen a few yards away.

"Let me see this gun of yours now. Easy and slow, if you please."

"What gun?" the driver asks innocently.

"The officer who arrested you said you had a gun in the glove compartment."

"There's no gun in there, see for yourself."

The sergeant opens the car door and has a look in the glove compartment. He finds nothing. He quickly walks to the back of the car and opens the boot.

"Er… why exactly are you looking in the boot, sir?" the guy asks.

"Well, I'll be damned. He called us saying that

there was this guy with no licence, no papers for the car, who had a gun and had used it to kill a man he kept hidden in the boot," the sergeant says, baffled.

"Oh. I see," replies the driver. "He's a rookie, is he?"

"Yes."

"And I bet he said I was speeding too, right?"

* * *

A guy is just keeping up with the traffic, not realising that by doing so he's breaking the speed limit. What's supposed to happen happens, and he gets caught by a mobile camera.

When the police pull him over, he's got his defence ready.

"OK, I know I was speeding, but there were plenty of cars driving just as fast as I did, so why didn't you arrest them?"

"Ever been fishing?" the policeman asked him urbanely.

"Yeah, a couple of times. Why?"

"Did you ever catch them all?"

* * *

A car is stopped by police near Dover. The driver rolls down the window and asks, "What's the problem, officer? I wasn't speeding, was I?"

"No, you weren't speeding. In fact, I've been following you for some time, and I'd like to congratulate you on your driving. You've been indicating all the time, you've been respecting the speed limits all through town… your driving is exemplary. You know, people always think of us as here to make drivers' lives miserable and give tickets. What very few people know is that we can also reward good drivers, too. This is why I stopped you. I'd like to reward you with a £500 cheque to encourage you to carry on driving the way you do."

"This is grand," the guy smiles. "Now I can get my licence."

"I told you we shouldn't have stolen this car," says his mate on the passenger seat.

"Don't pay any attention to him," the woman at the back says with a little nervous laugh. "He's always trying to be funny when he's on crack."

"Why are we stopping?" comes a voice from

inside the boot. "Have we come through the Channel Tunnel yet?"

* * *

Late one Friday night, a policeman spots a man driving very erratically through the streets of London. He pulls the man over and asks him if he's been drinking.

"Well, of course I've been drinking," the man says in a somewhat slurry speech. "It's Friday, and I always drink on Friday. You know what? There's not a decent pub to go to on a Friday night in Dalston. That's why I've got to drive all the way here. Me and me mate had a few beers, as usual, then we switched to whisky. They have a 'buy three, get the fourth one free' offer. I mean, I wasn't gonna let that pass, right? I get paid on Friday night but that doesn't mean I can't be careful about my money, eh? Then I met a couple of mates from work, and we had a few more rounds for the road and here I am."

The policeman sighs and says to the guy, "I'm sorry, sir. You'll have to take a breathalyser test."

"What? You don't believe me?" the driver asks indignantly.

* * *

Tom and Harry are having a great time in the car.
The radio's blaring, they're going to a party and
the night is young. They're also taking swigs from
a four-pack of bottled lager at regular intervals.
They're enjoying themselves so much, in fact,
that they don't see the speed camera and they get
flashed. In the distance, they now see the tell-tale
blue lights.

"Damn!" Tom swears. "Tell you what. Rip off the
labels from the bottles, stick them on our foreheads
and let me do the talking."

Harry, quite inebriated, does as he is told. He
sticks a label of 1664 on his forehead and one on
Tom's and hides the evidence under the seat.

"Good evening, gentlemen," says the policeman.
"You've been caught driving at 65 and this is a 50
zone."

"I'm sorry, officer," Tom replies contritely. "We're
on our way to a party and we're a bit late. I guess I
wasn't paying attention."

The policeman looks at him and says in a
suspicious tone, "Have you been drink-driving?"

Tom points at the label on his forehead and says, "No, officer. We've quit. We're on the patch."

* * *

John and Jessica are on their way home from the bar one night, when John gets pulled over by the police.

"Good evening, sir," says the officer. "It appears that your back light doesn't work."

"I'm very sorry, officer, I didn't realise it was out. I'll get it fixed right away," John says with a contrite smile.

Just then, Jessica says, "I knew this would happen. I told you two days ago to get that light fixed."

The officer squints sternly at John and asks to see the car's papers. After having examined the papers thoroughly, the policeman says, "Sir, your MOT has expired."

John apologises nervously and says he didn't realise it had expired, and he'll take care of it first thing in the morning.

Just then Jessica says, "I told you a week ago that the MOT was due. I even asked you if you wanted to get it booked with a garage but you never answered."

John grinds his teeth, quite upset with his wife contradicting him in front of the officer.

"Jessica, shut your mouth!" he says to her between clenched teeth.

The officer then leans over towards Jessica and asks, "Does your husband always talk to you like that?"

"Oh, no. Only when he's drunk." Jessica replies.

* * *

A woman and a man are involved in a really nasty car accident. Both their cars are totally demolished, but neither of them is hurt. After they crawl out of their cars, the woman says, "So you're a man – that's interesting. I'm a woman. Wow, just look at our cars! There's nothing left, but we're unhurt. This must be a sign from God that we should meet, get acquainted and live together in peace for the rest of our days."

The man feels great at having such good luck, so says, "Oh, yes, I agree with you completely! This must be a sign from the Lord!"

The woman continues, "And look at this – another miracle. My car is demolished, but this bottle of wine didn't break. Surely God wants us to drink this wine and celebrate our good fortune."

She hands the bottle to the man, who nods his head in agreement, opens the bottle and drinks half of it before handing it back to the woman. The woman takes the bottle and immediately puts the cap back on.

The man asks, "Aren't you having any?"

The woman replies, "No. I think I'll just wait for the police!"

Women are clever. Don't mess with them.

* * *

Brother William is on his way back from teaching children at a local school. It is late at night, and the Abbey's car that he is travelling in breaks down. He knows he hasn't run out of petrol because he just filled up, so he opens up the bonnet and starts to have a look at the engine.

A few minutes later, a car pulls up next to him and the window is wound down. A red-faced chap pops his head out and says, "Hello old chap, what's the matter with you then?"

"Piston broke I think," says the monk, to which the man in the car replies, "Me too, but what's up with the motor?"

* * *

After passing his driving test, Davey comes home and says, "Dad, can I use the car?"

His dad replies, "OK, son, but first you have to mow the lawn every week for three months and get your hair cut."

Three months pass, and Davey comes into the house and says, "Dad, the lawn's looked like Lords for the last three months. How about letting me use the car now?"

The dad replies, "That's true. But, son, you didn't cut your hair."

So Davey says, "But, Dad, Jesus had long hair!"

"You're right," says Davey's dad. "And he walked everywhere."

A girl was driving down the A13,
when her car phone rang.
It was her boyfriend, urgently warning
her, "I just heard on the news that there's
a car going the wrong way on the A13.
Please be careful!"
"It's not just one car!" said the girl.
"There's hundreds of them!"

* * *

A woman had been driving 16 hours straight, when
she decided she'd had enough; she was still at least
six hours away from her destination, it was almost
seven o'clock in the morning and she had dozed off,
nearly crashing into a telegraph pole. She decided
to pull on to a side road and rest for a bit before
carrying on. She turned off the car and closed her
eyes... drifting off to sleep, precious sleep... When
an old man in a bright blue jogging suit knocked
on her window, scaring her half to death.

"Sorry to wake you," he huffed, jogging in place.
"But can you tell me what time it is?"

The woman glanced at her watch. "7:15," she said through the glass.

"Thank you," the jogger said, and left.

"Just my luck," the woman muttered angrily. "I'm parked on someone's jogging route."

She considered driving off and parking somewhere else, but she was too tired, so she settled back into the seat, trying to recapture the beautiful dream she was having… When another jogger knocked on her window.

"Hi, do you have the time?" he said.

The woman sighed and looked at her watch. "7:19," she said. "Thanks," the jogger said, then trotted off.

She looked down the road and saw more joggers coming her way. Irritated, she retrieved a pen from the glove box and scrawled "I DO NOT KNOW THE TIME" on the back of a magazine. She jammed the hastily-constructed sign in the window with her shoulder and settled back to sleep.

A jogger knocked on the window just as she started dozing off. The woman pointed at the sign and shouted, "Can't you read?"

"Sure I can, ma'am. I just wanted to let you know… it's 7:27."

* * *

Did you hear about the wooden car with wooden seats, wooden bodywork, wooden wheels and a wooden engine? Wooden go!

* * *

A woman stops at a red light behind a trucker. She leaps out of her car, knocks on his window and says, "Hi, my name's Cheryl and you're losing your load."

The trucker shakes his head and drives on. At the next set of traffic lights, she stops behind him, gets out and taps on his window again saying, "Hi, I dunno if you heard me. My name's Cheryl and you're losing your load."

He drives on. At the third set of lights, she's still tapping on his window saying, "Hi, mate, my name's Cheryl and you're losing your load."

Once again, he shakes his head and drives on.

At the fourth set of lights, the truck driver leaps out of his cab quickly, goes over to the woman's car, taps on her window and says, "Hi, Cheryl. My name's Dave and I'm driving a gritter."

* * *

A taxi passenger tapped the driver on the shoulder to ask him a question. The driver screamed, lost control of the car and stopped just centimetres from a shop window.

The driver turned around and said, "Look, mate, don't do that again. You scared the daylights out of me!" The passenger apologized, and said he didn't realise that a tap on the shoulder could scare the driver so much. The driver replied, "Sorry, it's not your fault, mate. Today is my first day as a cab driver – I've been driving hearses for the last 25 years."

* * *

A woman is trying to get back home, but she's caught in a really nasty blizzard. She remembers somebody having told her once that when such a thing happens the best thing to do is to wait for the snow plough to turn up, then follow it. So she waits for an hour and, finally, a snow plough arrives. Dutifully, she starts the engine and follows it. She follows it for half an hour, going round in circles behind it, when the driver of the snow plough comes down from his cabin and approaches her car.

"OK, I've finished with the Tesco car park, lady," he tells her. "Do you want to follow me next door to Homebase?"

* * *

A woman is trying to sell her old car, but she is having a lot of problems because it has almost 230,000 miles on the clock.

One day, she reveals the problem to her mate.

"There is a possibility to make the car easier to sell, but it's not legal," says her mate.

"That doesn't matter," replies the woman, "if I can sell the car."

"OK," says her mate. "Here's the address of a friend of mine. He owns a car repair shop. Tell him I sent you and he'll 'fix it'. Then you shouldn't have a problem anymore trying to sell your car."

The following weekend the woman makes the trip to the mechanic. About one month after that, her mate asks her, "Did you sell your car?"

"No," replies the woman. "Why should I? It only has 50,000 miles on the clock."

FOOD

This hunter has been chasing a deer for a whole day and comes back home with his prize, quite happy with himself. He decides to clean it and dress it, so that he can cook it the following day.

There's a strange aroma in the kitchen the following day, one the kids can't really place. It's strong and pungent and a bit meaty. Nonetheless, whatever's being cooked is placed on the table for the family to eat.

Overcome with curiosity and quite fussy about what he eats, the little boy asks his dad, "What are we eating today, dad?"

The dad smiles and says, "Well, let's say it's something your mum calls me sometimes."

The daughter looks at her brother in alarm.

"Don't eat it! It's an asshole!"

* * *

It is a well-known fact that if you drop a piece of toast, it will always land on the buttered side.

It is also a well-known fact that if you throw a cat in the air, it will always land on its paws.

Consequently, if one was to strap a piece of toast, butter-side up, to the back of a cat and throw the cat high in the air, one would have a perpetually hovering cat, according to the two laws described earlier.

* * *

A man walks into a restaurant and orders a cheeseburger.

Later, the waitress brings his meal to him. He takes a bite out of it and notices there's a small hair in the hamburger. He begins yelling frantically at the waitress, "Waitress, there's a hair in my hamburger! I demand to see what's going on!"

So the waitress takes him to the kitchen and, to his horror, he sees the cook take the meat patty and flatten it under his armpit. He says, "That's disgusting!"

The waitress replies, "You think that's disgusting? You should see him make doughnuts."

* * *

A Jelly Baby goes to the
doctor. "Doctor, doctor;
I think I've got an STD."
The doctor is surprised,
"You can't have an STD,
you're a Jelly Baby!"
"But, doctor, I've been
sleeping with Allsorts."

* * *

A customer at Morris' Gourmet Grocery marvelled
at the proprietor's quick wit and intelligence.

"Tell me, Morris, what makes you
so smart?"

"I wouldn't share my secret with just anyone,"
Morris replies, lowering his voice so the other
shoppers won't hear, "but, since you're a good
and faithful customer, I'll let you in on it. Fish
heads: you eat enough of them, you'll be positively
brilliant."

"You sell them here?" the customer asks.

"Only £4 apiece," says Morris.

The customer buys three. A week later, he's back

in the store complaining that the fish heads were disgusting, and that he isn't any smarter.

"You didn't eat enough," says Morris.

The customer goes home with 20 more fish heads. Two weeks later, he's back and this time he's really angry.

"Hey, Morris," he says, "you're selling me fish heads for £4 apiece, when I just found out I can buy the whole fish for £2. You're ripping me off!"

"You see?" says Morris. "You're smarter already."

* * *

What contains two egg sandwiches and a Kit Kat, and hangs around French cathedrals?
The lunch pack of Notre Dame.

* * *

What sort of meringues can you never throw away?
Boomeringues.

* * *

After watching a program about the Egyptians on TV, a woman decides to treat herself to a milk bath. She leaves a note to the milkman which reads, "30 litres of milk tomorrow, please."

On finding the note in the morning, the milkman is a bit confused and knocks on the door.

"You mean three litres, right?"

"No, you read right, 30 litres, please," the woman smiles back.

"Er… OK. Pasteurised?"

"No, just up to my tits."

* * *

A man orders a pizza. When it is done, the cook asks him, "Do you want me to cut it into six or twelve pieces?"

"Six, please," he says, "I couldn't eat twelve."

A resident in a posh hotel breakfast room calls over the head waiter one morning.

"Good morning, sir," says the waiter. "What would you like for breakfast today?"

"I'd like two boiled eggs, one of them so undercooked it's runny and the other so overcooked it's tough and hard to eat. Also, grilled bacon that has been left out so it gets a bit on the cold side; burnt toast that crumbles away as soon as you touch it with a knife; butter straight from the deep freeze so that it's impossible to spread and a pot of very weak coffee, lukewarm."

"That's a complicated order, sir," said the bewildered waiter. "It might be quite difficult."

The guest replied, "Oh? I don't understand why. That's exactly what I got yesterday."

* * *

What's the difference between roast beef and pea soup?
Anyone can roast beef.

* * *

A man goes into a fish 'n' chip shop with a salmon under his arm.
He asks, "Do you sell fish cakes here?"
"No," comes the reply.
"Shame, it's his birthday."

* * *

A man and woman go on date to an Italian restaurant. They arrive, order and the woman disappears to the toilet. The man waits for five minutes, but there's still no sign of the woman. He is still waiting for her 20 minutes later when the food has arrived.

Finally, after half an hour, she eventually comes back to find the man squeezing the pasta on his plate.

"What on earth do you think you are doing!" she screams in disgust.

"I was feeling cannelloni," he replies.

* * *

Riding the favourite at Cheltenham, a jockey is well ahead of the field. Suddenly, he is hit on the head by a turkey and a string of sausages.

He manages to stay on his mount and pull back into the lead, only to be struck by a box of Christmas crackers and a dozen mince pies over the last fence.

He again manages to regain the lead, when he's hit by a bottle of sherry full in the face.

Eventually, he comes in second. Furious, he goes to the stewards' room to complain that he has been seriously hampered.

HEALTH

A woman spots a little old man sitting happily on a park bench and wanders over for a chat.

"I can't help but notice how happy you look," she says. "What's your secret?"

"Well," replies the man, "I smoke, drink, eat junk food all day and don't exercise..."

"Wow!" replies the woman. "How old are you?"

"Twenty-three."

* * *

A man walks into a doctor's office. "What seems to be the problem?" asks the doc.

"It's... um... well... I have five willies," replies the man.

"Blimey!" says the doctor. "How do your trousers fit?"

"Like a glove."

A bloke hasn't been feeling well, so he goes for a complete check-up. Afterwards the doctor comes out with the results.

"I'm afraid I have some very bad news," says the doctor. "You're dying, and you don't have much time left."

"That's terrible," says the bloke. "How long have I got?"

"Ten," the doctor says sadly.

"Ten?" the bloke asks. "Ten what? Months? Weeks? What?"

"Nine... Eight..."

* * *

A bloke goes to see the doctor after a sudden illness. He takes his wife with him and, after a thorough examination, the doctor asks if he could speak to the wife for a moment.

The bloke leaves the room while the doctor tells the wife the bad news.

"Your husband has a rare condition – any form of bad news or stress could instantly kill him, so you must cater to his every whim. Make him breakfast, lunch and dinner. Make love to him whenever he requires. Don't tell him off about anything at all. Is that understood?"

The wife nods and then leaves to join her husband.

Once outside the bloke asks his wife, "What did the doctor say?"

She replies solemnly, "He said you're going to die very soon."

* * *

Shaun is ill. He goes to see his GP, who prescribes a suppository.

"You take this via the rectum," he tells him.

Shaun acquiesces, although he doesn't have a clue what a rectum is. Puzzled, he goes and sees a friend.

"Say, do you know what a rectum is?"

"Nope."

After two hours spent driving around his friends asking the same question – and getting the same answer – Shaun gives up and goes back home. He gets a glass of water and simply swallows the damn pill. Two weeks later, he goes back to his GP.

"So, did you see any improvement with your treatment?"

"Aw, no," Shaun says. "It didn't work. I could have shoved this pill right up my backside and it wouldn't have been any better!"

* * *

A man goes to the doctor and says, "Doctor, I'm having some trouble with my hearing."
"What are the symptoms?" asks the doctor.
The man replies, "A yellow TV cartoon family."

* * *

An old feller with a dodgy heart goes to see his doctor about some chest pains he's been experiencing. When he gets home, his wife asks him if he's been prescribed medication.

"No, nothing like that," says the old man. "I'm going to make some lunch."

Wanting to give him some space, the wife lets her husband go. Ten minutes later, she hears screams of pain coming from the kitchen and rushes in to find the old guy cooking a fry-up in a biscuit tin and burning his fingers whenever he touches it.

"What on earth are you doing?" she screams.

"Just following doctor's orders," says the old man. "He said the best thing I can do for my heart is to throw away the frying pan."

* * *

A bloke goes to the doctor's and complains that he can't do all the things around the house that he used to do.

When the examination is complete, the bloke says, "Now, Doc, I can take it. Tell me in plain English what's wrong with me."

"Well, in plain English," replies the doctor, "you're just lazy."

"OK," says the bloke. "Now give me the medical term so I can tell my wife."

* * *

A man is lying in bed in the hospital with an oxygen mask over his mouth. A young nurse appears to sponge his hands and feet.

"Excuse me, nurse," he mumbles from behind the mask, "are my testicles black?"

Embarrassed, the young nurse replies, "I don't know. I'm only here to give you a bed-bath."

He struggles again to ask, "Nurse, are my testicles black?"

Finally, she pulls back the covers, raises his gown and gives him a thorough examination before saying, "No. There doesn't seem to be anything wrong with them."

Finally, the man pulls off his oxygen mask and replies, "That was very nice, but are... my... test... results... back?"

* * *

An old gamekeeper was walking round the estate with the lord of the manor. His Lordship was surprised and a bit disgusted to see the gamekeeper reach over into the cow's field as they walked past, grab a handful of dung and rub it on his lips.

"What on earth did you do that for?" asked his Lordship.

"Got chapped lips from this cold weather," said the old gamekeeper.

"And does that stuff heal them?" asked his Lordship.

"Not exactly," said the old man, "but it sure stops me lickin' em."

* * *

An old man goes to the doctor and says, "Doctor, I have this problem with farting, but it really doesn't bother me too much. They never smell and are always silent. As a matter of fact, I've farted at least 20 times since I've been here in your office. You didn't know I was passing gas, you see, because, as I say, they're odourless and noiseless."

The doctor says, "I see. Take these pills and come back to see me next week."

The next week the man goes back. "Doctor," he says, "I don't know what the heck you gave me, but now when I fart they're still silent but they stink terribly."

"Good," the doctor says. "Now that we've cleared up your sinuses, let's get to work on your hearing."

* * *

A man is sitting watching TV one evening when the bell rings. Surprised, because he wasn't expecting anyone, the guy goes to answer the door and finds himself nose to nose with a six-foot cockroach. The cockroach looks him up and down and, without warning, punches him in the nose.

Utterly flabbergasted, the guy doesn't have time to react and the cockroach is gone before he can retaliate.

Back in the house, nursing his bloody nose, the guy hears the doorbell again. He cautiously opens the door and is confronted by the same cockroach, who kicks him solidly between the legs, before scampering away, laughing maniacally.

Curled on the sofa, blood dripping from his nose, the guy is feeling sorry for himself and is just about to get a swig from a now-warm can of beer, when the doorbell rings again. Grabbing a walking stick, the guy pugnaciously swings the door open, only to have the same cockroach fire at him with a pepper-spray gun. While he's on the floor in tears, the cockroach smacks him with a baseball bat and drives both his elbows into each of the guy's kidneys, before running off howling.

Crawling back into the living room, the poor guy calls the hospital. The ambulance crew turns up a few minutes later, and he explains to them what happened, what with the six-foot cockroach and the baseball bat and the pepper spray and all.

The paramedic only nods in sympathy and says, "Yeah, we know. There's a nasty bug going around."

IT

Two IT guys were walking across the park one day, when they spotted a colleague riding a brand-new bike.

"Where did you get such a great bike?" they marvelled.

The third guy replied, "Well, I was walking along yesterday minding my own business, when a beautiful woman rode up on this bike. She threw the bike to the ground, took off all her clothes and said, 'Take what you want, big boy!'"

The first IT guy nodded approvingly, "Good choice. The clothes probably wouldn't have fit."

* * *

An architect, an artist and an IT guy were discussing whether it was better to have a wife or a mistress. The architect said he enjoyed his time with his wife, building a solid foundation for an enduring relationship. The artist said he enjoyed time with his mistress, because of the passion and mystery he found there.

The IT guy said, "I like both."

The artist said, "Both? Isn't that a bit excessive?"

The IT guy replied, "Yeah, but if you have a wife and a mistress, they will each assume you are spending time with the other woman, so you can sneak off to the office and get some work done."

LAWYERS AND THE LAW

At the funeral of a lady were her doctor, a friend and her lawyer. Each had promised her that at her funeral they would toss £1000 into her grave. The doctor and friend each tossed in their £1000 cash, after which the lawyer removed the cash and placed a cheque for £3000.

* * *

Prosecutor: "Did you kill the victim?"

Defendant: "No, I did not."

Prosecutor: "Do you know what the penalties are for perjury?"

Defendant: "Yes, I do. And they're a hell of a lot better than the penalty for murder."

* * *

A rich lawyer is approached by a charity for a donation. The man from the charity is concerned that the lawyer makes over £1,000,000 a year but doesn't give a penny to good causes.

"First of all," says the lawyer, "my mother is sick and dying in the hospital, and it's not covered by insurance. Second, I have five kids from three failed marriages. Third, my sister's husband suddenly died, and she has no one to support her four children."

"I'm terribly sorry," says the charity man. "I feel bad about asking for money."

The lawyer responds, "Yeah, well, if I'm not giving them anything, why should you get any?"

* * *

A farmer is in court fighting for a large insurance claim following a serious road accident he didn't cause. He is being questioned by the insurance company's lawyer and is being given a hard time because of his conflicting statements.

The lawyer asks, "So, Farmer Brown. You are trying to claim substantial damages from the person you claim caused the accident, yet I have a sworn statement from the police officer who was present at the scene claiming that when asked how you were feeling immediately following the accident, you said, and I quote, 'I'm fine, officer; in fact, I've never felt better in my life!'"

There is a gasp around the courtroom.

"Now, is this or is this not true, Farmer Brown?" continues the brief.

"Well, yes, but…," the farmer starts, but he is interrupted by the barrister.

"Just a simple yes or no answer will suffice, Farmer Brown."

"Yes," says Farmer Brown.

After a while, it was the turn of the lawyer for the farmer's insurance to question him.

"So, Farmer Brown, tell us the exact circumstances surrounding your statement of good health that my learned friend just made you discuss," the barrister says to the farmer.

"Well, sir, as I was trying to say," Farmer Brown explains, "I had just had this horrific accident, and I was lying in the middle of the road injured. My horse had been injured too, and so had my dog. So, after a little while a policeman comes up to the horse, sees it struggling for life and shoots it. Then he walks over to my dog, hears it howling and shoots it. Then he walks over to me, bleeding on the floor, and says, 'How are you, sir?' Now what the hell would you have said in those circumstances?"

* * *

A defence lawyer says to his client, "I've got good news and bad news. The bad news is your blood test came back, and the DNA is an exact match with the sample found on the victim's shirt." "Damn," says the client. "What's the good news?" "Your cholesterol is down to 140."

* * *

Two physicians boarded a flight out of Seattle. One sat in the window seat, the other sat in the middle seat. Just before takeoff, an attorney got on and took the aisle seat next to the two physicians. The attorney kicked off his shoes, wiggled his toes and was settling in when the physician in the window seat said, "I think I'll get up and get a coke."

"No problem," said the attorney, "I'll get it for you."

While he was gone, one of the physicians picked up the attorney's shoe and spat in it. When he returned with the coke, the other physician said, "That looks good, I think I'll have one, too."

Again, the attorney obligingly went to fetch it and while he was gone, the other physician picked up the other shoe and spat in it. The attorney returned and they all sat back and enjoyed the flight. As the plane was landing, the attorney slipped his feet into his shoes and knew immediately what had happened.

"How long must this go on?" he asked. "This fighting between our professions? This hatred? This animosity? This spitting in shoes and pissing in cokes?"

* * *

A man goes into a lawyer's office and says, "I heard people have sued tobacco companies for giving them lung cancer."

The lawyer says, "Yes, that's perfectly true."

The man says, "Well, I'm interested in suing someone, too."

The lawyer says, "OK. Who are you talking about?"

The man replies, "I'd like to sue all the breweries for the ugly women I've slept with."

* * *

On trial in a rural American town, an English man thinks he has no chance of getting off a murder charge, despite his innocence. So, shortly before the jury retires, he bribes one of the jurors to find him guilty of the lesser crime of manslaughter.

The jury is out for over three days, before eventually returning a verdict of manslaughter.

The relieved defendant collars the bribed juror and says, "Thanks. However did you manage it?"

"It wasn't easy," admits the juror. "All the others wanted to acquit you."

A young entrepreneur starts his own business. He is shrewd and diligent, so business keeps coming in. Pretty soon he realises that he needs an in-house counsel, and so he begins interviewing young lawyers.

"As I'm sure you can understand," he starts off with one of the first applicants, "in a business like this, our personal integrity must be beyond question." He leans forward. "Mr. Peterson, are you an 'honest' lawyer?"

"Honest?" replies the job prospect. "Let me tell you something about honesty. I'm so honest that my dad lent me £15,000 for my education, and I paid back every penny the minute I completed my very first case."

"Impressive. And what sort of case was that?"

"My father filed a small claims suit against me."

* * *

One afternoon, a wealthy lawyer is riding in the back of his limousine when he sees two men eating grass by the roadside. He orders his driver to stop and gets out to investigate.

"Why are you eating grass?" he asks one man.

"We don't have any money for food," the poor man replies.

"Oh, come along with me then."

"But sir, I have a wife with two children!"

"Bring them along! And you, come with us too!" he says to the other man.

"But sir, I have a wife with six children!" the second man answers.

"Bring them as well!"

They all climb into the car, which was no easy task, even for a car as large as the limo. Once under way, one of the poor fellows says, "Sir, you are too kind. Thank you for taking all of us with you."

The lawyer replies, "No problem. The grass at my home is about two feet tall!

* * *

A London lawyer is representing a local train company in a lawsuit filed by a West Country farmer. The farmer's prize bull is missing from the section of field through which the railway passes. The farmer wants to be paid the market price for the bull and, just before the case, the lawyer immediately corners the farmer and tries to get him to settle out of court. The lawyer does his best selling job, and finally the farmer agrees to take half of what he was asking.

After the farmer signs the release and takes his pay-off, the young lawyer can't resist gloating a little over his success.

Outside the High Court he shakes the farmer's hand and tells him, "You know, I hate to tell you this, old feller, but I put one over on you in there. I couldn't have won the case. The driver was asleep when the train went through your farm that morning. I didn't have one witness to put on the stand. I bluffed you!"

The rosy-cheeked farmer replies, "Well, I'll tell you, boy, I was a little worried about winning that case myself, because I'll be blowed if that bull didn't come home this morning."

* * *

What's the difference between a
bad lawyer and a good lawyer?
A bad lawyer can let a case drag
on for months.
A good lawyer can make it last
for years.

* * *

A man has been charged with fraud and is now facing the
judge. His lawyer, a thoroughly arrogant man, makes his
way over to the judge and waves a chequebook.

"He's guilty. I know this, you know this, so let's
make it short and I'll write the bail cheque."

The judge looks him up and down and replies,
"You'll have ample time to present your case later on.
For now, let's follow the correct procedure."

"A man of the financial stature of my client doesn't
have time for procedure. Just give me the amount
and I'll write the cheque."

"Very well," the judge replies, a steely glint in his
eyes. "Please write me out a cheque for six months'
imprisonment."

LEISURE ACTIVITIES

A guy is diving for fun and has reached 15 metres when he sees another man, without any scuba gear on whatsoever. Puzzled, he gives the guy a wave and goes down an extra five metres. A minute later, the same guy's there, still with no scuba gear on.

Astonished, the diver picks up his slate and writes, "How the hell do you manage to dive without scuba gear?"

The guy reads the plate, erases it and writes, "I'm drowning, you moron!"

* * *

Two guys are golfing on a course that is right next to a cemetery. After they tee off, one of the golfers notices that there is a funeral procession sombrely passing by. He takes off his hat, and places it over his heart.

When the funeral is over, the other golfer asks, "Why did you do that?"

The man replies, "Well, we were married for almost 40 years. It's the least I could do."

* * *

A man tells his wife after work, "Honey, I have the opportunity to go fishing for a week in Scotland, all free, paid by the company as part of a staff development scheme."

"That's pretty good," the wife says.

"I kind of have to go, really," the husband carries on. "All my colleagues will be there, and my boss too. Ladder of success and Brownie points, you know…"

"Yes, this would be a great opportunity for you to get to know him better, so that you can ask for a pay rise later on. Go for it."

"Thanks, honey. Can you pack my bag? Put my blue pyjamas in."

The wife dutifully packs his bag, and the guy is off for a week's fishing.

When he comes back, his wife asks him if he's had a good time.

"Oh, it was great, but you forgot my blue pyjamas."

"I didn't," his wife replies sweetly. "I put them in your tackle box."

This bloke goes to the Cup Final and notices that there's an empty seat between him and the next spectator.

"Imagine that," he comments. "Someone had a ticket for the most important game of the year and didn't turn up."

The guy next to him explains that the seat was for his wife, that every year they went to the final together, but she had died and this was the first time he'd gone on his own.

"That's awful!" says the first guy. "Couldn't you have got a friend or relative to come with you?"

"No," he replies. "Everyone I know is at the funeral."

* * *

A golfer is about to tee off when he's approached by a man holding out a card that reads, "I am a deaf mute. May I please play through?"

The guy gives the card back, angrily shaking his head. Assuming the guy can lip-read, he adds, "I can't believe you would try to use your handicap for a cheap advantage like that! Of course you can't play through!"

The deaf man walks away, and the guy whacks the ball on to the green and then walks off to finish the hole.

Just as the golfer is about to putt out, he's hit in the head with a golf ball that knocks him out cold.

When he comes to a few minutes later, he looks around and sees the deaf mute sternly looking at him, one hand on his driver, the other hand holding up four fingers.

* * *

At half-time during a football match, the coach says to one of his young players, "Do you understand what cooperation is? What a team is?"

The little boy nods in the affirmative.

"Do you understand that what matters is whether we win together as a team?"

The little boy nodded yes again.

"So," the coach continued, "when you have to go forward or move right, you do it. You don't argue and don't insult the referee. Do you understand?"

Again the little boy nodded.

"Good," said the coach, "now go over there and explain it to your mother.'

* * *

This guy is at the bar above a pool club. He looks thoroughly dejected and is sinking beer after beer. A fellow player comes to sit next to him and asks him what's up.

"Well, I had a bet with this guy," he says glumly. "He asked me for a game, and he said I'd lose it, however many frames I did."

"So?"

"So I asked how many frames he'd win by, and he said he just needed two gotchas."

"What on earth is a gotcha?"

"That's what I asked but all he said was, 'You'll see'."

The guy buys him another beer and his friend continues.

"So, here I was, carefully placing the balls, concentrating, and ready to put the red in the pocket, when suddenly he screams 'Gotcha!'"

"Oh! I guess that was a bit of a surprise."

"You can say that again. It threw me off totally. I missed the shot and nearly ripped the cloth off the table."

"Still, that's only one shot. He said he needed two."

"Yeah, well. Have you got any idea how hard it is to play when you're expecting the next gotcha?"

* * *

A pastor, a doctor and an engineer are playing golf and are waiting at a hole for the group ahead to finish. They are waiting and waiting, until it gets too much for the engineer, who goes to have a look and ask the players to hurry up a bit.

He comes back to his fellow-golfers with some sad news.

"It's a small group of blind firemen," he explains. "They were out on a call last month, when the building blew up. The club is letting them play out of charity."

"How sad," the priest says. "We should say a prayer of thanks to the Lord for having spared them."

"How sad indeed," the doctor agreed. "I have a friend, he's a renowned ophthalmologist. Maybe he can do something for them."

"Yeah, well, why can't they play at night?" the engineer grumbles.

What's the difference between a bad golfer and a bad skydiver?
The golfer goes, "Thump... DAMN!"

A caddy has been around the course today and has picked up a fair number of golf balls. He shares the load equally in his pockets and walks to the bus stop. At the door of the bus, he has to fumble in his pockets to find some change. In doing so, he puts all the balls from his left pocket into his right.

Finally, he pays the driver and goes to sit near an old lady. Unfortunately, all these balls in his right pocket make his sitting a bit uncomfortable, and he keeps on squirming and fidgeting, trying to find a comfortable position.

"Is something the matter, dear?" the old lady next to him asks.

"Oh, it's nothing," the caddy replies and then explains, "golf balls.'

"Oh, I see. Is that a bit like tennis elbow?" the old woman asks innocently.

A priest is off playing golf on a Sunday. When he woke up this morning the sun was shining, the air was crisp and he just couldn't let that pass; he's been wanting to play for ages. So he phones a friend of his, also a priest, and asks for a favour, and here he is now, concentrating on his swing. The birds are singing, the air smells of pine and freshly-cut grass and an angel leans over to whisper in God's ear, "He's deliberately lying to his flock! You can't let him get away with that!"

God hushes the angel and watches as the priest swings.

The golf ball arcs across the sky in a perfect parabola, with majesty and grace, and lands on the green, 250 yards away, where it gently rolls towards the flag and finally plops into the hole.

"A 250-yard hole-in-one putt? You can't let him get away with it!" the angel gasps.

"And why not? Who's he gonna tell?" chuckles God.

MAGIC

A woman finds an old lamp in the attic, and when she polishes, it a genie pops out offering to grant her three wishes. However, he warns her that whatever she wishes for, the bloke in her life will get ten times better or more.

So the woman thinks about this and says, "For my first wish I'd like to be the most beautiful woman in the world."

The genie says, "OK, but remember your bloke will be the most handsome man in the world and every woman will lust after him."

The woman replies, "Go ahead." So sure enough she's the world's most beautiful woman.

"For my second wish I want to be the richest woman in the world."

The genie warns, "That will make your bloke ten times richer than you."

"Fine by me," comes the reply. So she's the richest woman in the world.

The genie asks, "What is your final wish?"

Her reply is, "I'd like a very mild heart attack!"

* * *

A man finds a genie in a bottle, and is offered three wishes.

First, he asks for a fast sports car. Suddenly, a Ferrari appears before him.

Next, he asks for a big house. Suddenly, he's sitting in a huge mansion.

Finally, he asks to be made irresistible to women. Suddenly, he turns into a box of luxury chocolates.

* * *

There was a woman who wanted to change her life.

She had tried everything to attract her husband's attention and praise, but he'd always shrugged her off and laughed at her. This had been going on for too long; she needed a change. She needed to dazzle her husband and have him admire her in some way, like he said he did ten years ago before turning into a couch potato, completely uninterested in whatever she did.

All this she explained to the pet shop owner, who replied, "I understand. You need something unusual, something unique, something that will impress your man. I have what you need."

He led her to the back of the store where a strange looking bird was standing forlornly on a wooden perch. The bird was half green, half yellow, had webbed feet and an enormous beak.

"He doesn't look like much but, believe me, this is an extraordinary bird," the owner continued. He then commanded the bird, "Goony bird! The shelf!"

As if voice-activated, the bird woke up from its torpor and dashed to the nearest shelf, smashing it to pieces with a few blows of its incredibly powerful beak. Once this was done, it returned to its perch and stood there just as before.

"This is incredible," the wife exclaimed. "I'm sure my husband would like it very much, it would be very useful to get rid of all the junk he's got piled up in the shed."

"All you have to do," the shopkeeper then explained, "is to say 'Goony Bird' and whatever you want it to smash to pieces."

Delighted, the woman took the bird home. To test the new pet, she took it to the shed and said, "Goony Bird! The old table!"

Instantly the bird flew to the old, dilapidated

table and proceeded to reduce it to a neat pile of splinters. The woman was over the moon.

"If that doesn't impress him, nothing will," she thought with a smile.

Holding the bird on its perch, she entered the house and came into the living room, where her husband was busy drinking beer and watching an inane program on TV.

"Darling! Look what I got for you! A Goony Bird!"

The husband, never taking his eyes from the screen, smirked, "Goony Bird? My ass!"

* * *

A sales rep, an administration clerk and their manager are walking to lunch, when they find an antique oil lamp. They rub it, and a genie comes out in a puff of smoke. The genie considers the situation and says, "I usually only grant three wishes, so I'll give each of you just one."

"Me first! Me first!" says the admin clerk. "I want to be in the Bahamas, driving a speedboat, without a care in the world."

Poof! She's gone.

In astonishment, "Me next! Me next!" says the sales rep. "I want to be in Hawaii, relaxing on the beach with my personal masseuse, an endless supply of pina coladas, and the love of my life."

Poof! He's gone.

"OK, you're up," the genie says to the manager.

The manager says, "I want those two back in the office after lunch."

Moral: Always let your boss have the first say.

* * *

There are two statues in a park, one of a nude man and one of a nude woman. They had been facing each other across a pathway for a hundred years, when one day an angel comes down from the sky and, with a single gesture, brings the two to life.

"As a reward for being so patient," says the angel, "you have been given life for 30 minutes to do what you've wished to do the most."

Immediately, the two statues disappear off behind a shrubbery. The angel waits patiently as the bushes rustle and giggling ensues until, after fifteen minutes, the two return out of breath.

The angel tells them, "Um, you have fifteen minutes left."

The male statue asks the female statue, "Shall we do it again?"

"Oh, yes," she replies. "But let's change positions. This time, I'll hold the pigeon down, and you crap on its head."

MEN AND WOMEN

* * *

Why do only ten per cent of men make it to heaven? Because if they all got there, it would be hell.

* * *

What has eight arms and an IQ of 60? Four guys watching a football match.

* * *

Why do most women pay more attention to their appearance than improving their minds?
Because most men are stupid, but not many are blind.

* * *

Things never to say to an excited, naked man:
This explains your car.
You know, they have surgery to fix that.
So, this is why you're supposed to judge people
on personality.
Is that an optical illusion?
Maybe if we water it, it'll grow.
Are you cold?
Wow – and your feet are so big!
I never saw one like that before.
Maybe it looks better in natural light.
Why don't we skip right to the cigarette?
Does it come with an air pump?

* * *

Why do men die before their wives?
They want to.

* * *

Why do women like to have
sex in the dark?
They can't stand seeing a man
have a good time.

*　*　*

How do men sort their dirty clothes?
"Dirty" and "dirty-but-wearable".

*　*　*

**Why is psychoanalysis quicker
for men than for women?
When it's time for regression,
men are already there.**

*　*　*

One day in a jewellery shop, a man is in the process of
buying a really expensive necklace with a lovely silver
locket on it.

The jeweller asks him, "Would you like her name
engraved on it?"

The man has a think and then replies, "No, just put
'To my one and only love.' That way, if we split up
and she throws it back in anger, I'll be able to recycle!"

*　*　*

**Did you hear the one about the
constipated mathematician?
He worked it out with a pencil.**

* * *

Why don't women blink
during foreplay?
They don't have enough time.

* * *

Did you hear about the streaker
who was thinking of retirement?
He decided to stick it out for one
more year!

* * *

**What has 100 balls
and screws old ladies?
Bingo.**

* * *

How do you make four old ladies
shout a four-letter word?
Get a fifth old lady to shout "Bingo!"

* * *

Why is sleeping with a man
like a soap opera?
Just when it's getting interesting, it's all
over until next time.

* * *

*What's the difference between a man
buying a lottery ticket and a man arguing
with his wife?
The man buying the ticket at least has
a one in 16,000,000 chance of winning!*

* * *

**What's the late-night difference between
a bachelor and a married man?**
A bachelor comes home, sees what's
in the refrigerator and goes to bed. A
married man comes home, sees what's in
the bed and goes to the refrigerator.

* * *

What do cookery books and science fiction have in common?

Men read them and think, "Well, that's not going to happen."

* * *

*Wife to husband: "Who was that lady
I seen you with last night?"
Husband: "You mean 'I saw.'"
Wife: "OK. Who was that eyesore
I seen you with last night?"*

* * *

A couple is lying in bed.

The man says, "I am going to make you the happiest woman in the world."

The woman says, "I'll miss you."

* * *

On the wall in the ladies' room: "My husband follows me everywhere..."
Written just below it: "No, I do not!"

* * *

He said: "Shall we try swapping positions tonight?"
She said: "That's a good idea... you stand by the ironing board and I'll sit on the sofa and fart."

* * *

He said: "What have you been doing with all the grocery money I gave you?"
She said: "Turn sideways and look in the mirror."

* * *

Jake was dying. His wife, Becky, was maintaining a candlelight vigil by his side. She held his fragile hand, tears running down her face. Her praying roused him from his slumber.

He looked up, and his pale lips began to move slightly, "My darling Becky," he whispered.

"Hush, my love," she said. "Rest. Shhh, don't talk."

He was insistent. "Becky," he said in his tired voice, "I have something I must confess to you."

"There's nothing to confess," replied the weeping Becky. "Everything's all right. Go to sleep."

"No, no, I must die in peace, Becky. I'm so sorry. I slept with your sister and your best friend. I slept with her best friend. I even slept with your mother!"

"I know," Becky whispered softly. "That's why I poisoned you."

* * *

Why is it so difficult to find men who are sensitive, caring and good-looking? They already have boyfriends.

* * *

Mary Clancy goes up to Father O'Grady after his Sunday morning service, and she's in tears. He says, "So what's bothering you, Mary my dear?"

She says, "Oh, Father, I've got terrible news. My husband passed away last night."

The priest says, "Oh, Mary, that's terrible. Tell me, Mary, did he have any last requests?"

She says, "That he did, Father."

The priest says, "What did he ask, Mary?"

She says, "He said, 'Please Mary, put down that damn gun...'"

* * *

A man is dining in a fancy restaurant and there is a gorgeous redhead sitting at the next table. He has been checking her out since he sat down, but lacks the nerve to talk with her. Suddenly, she sneezes and her glass eye comes flying out of its socket towards the man. He reflexively reaches out, grabs it out of the air and hands it back.

"Oh my, I am sooo sorry," the woman says as she pops her eye back in place. "Let me buy your dinner to make it up to you," she says.

They enjoy a wonderful dinner together and afterwards the theatre followed by drinks. They talk, they laugh, she shares her deepest dreams and he shares his. After paying for everything, she asks him if he would like to come to her place for an intimate nightcap... and stay for breakfast the next morning. The next morning, she cooks a gourmet meal with all the trimmings.

The guy is amazed! Everything had been incredible. "You know," he said, "you are the perfect woman. Are you this nice to every guy you meet?"

"No," she replies. "You just happened to catch my eye."

* * *

What's the difference between a new husband and a new dog?
The dog is still excited to see you a year later.

Bob is sitting at the coffee shop, staring morosely into his cappuccino. Tom walks in and sits down. After trying to start a conversation several times and getting only distracted grunts, he asks Bob what the problem is.

"Well," says Bob, "I think I've upset my wife after she asked me one of those questions she always asks. Now I'm in deep trouble at home."

"What kind of question was it?"

"Well, my wife asked me if I would still love her when she was old, fat and ugly."

"That's easy," said Tom. "You just say, 'Of course I will!'"

"Yeah," said Bob, "that's what I did. Except I said, 'Of course I do'."

* * *

What do you call a woman who works as hard as a man? Lazy.

* * *

At the gates of heaven, God decides to put in a personal appearance and says, "I want the men to make two lines: one line for the men who were true heads of their households, and the other line for the men who were dominated by their women. I want all the women to report to St Peter."

Soon, the women are gone and there are two lines of men. The line of men who were dominated by their wives is 100 miles long, and in the line of men who truly were heads of their household, there is only one man.

God says, "You men should be ashamed of yourselves. I created you to be the head of your household. You have been disobedient and not fulfilled your purpose. I told you to be the spiritual leader in your family. Of all of you, only one obeyed. Learn from him! Tell them, my son, how did you manage to be the only one in this line?"

The man replies, "I don't know. My wife told me to stand here."

A woman walks into a gun shop and asks the salesman if he can help her pick out a rifle.

"It's for my husband," she explains.

"Did he tell you what calibre to get?" asks the salesman.

"Are you kidding? He doesn't even know I'm going to shoot him."

* * *

A man approaches a beautiful woman in a supermarket and asks, "You know, I've lost my wife here in the supermarket. Can you talk to me for a couple of minutes?"

"Why?" she asks.

"Because every time I talk to a beautiful woman, my wife appears out of nowhere."

* * *

A woman went to her psychiatrist because she was having problems with her sex life. The psychiatrist asked her many questions. Finally, he asked, "Do you ever watch your husband's face while you're having sex?"

"Well, yes, I actually did once," replied the woman.

"And tell me, how did your husband look?" asked the psychiatrist.

"Angry. Fuming, actually," replied the woman.

At this point, the psychiatrist felt that he was getting somewhere and said, "Well, that's interesting. How did it occur that you saw his face that time?"

"He was looking at me through the window!"

* * *

Four blokes are making the most of a fine Sunday with a round of golf. During the fourth hole they discuss how they actually got away from their wives for the day.

First bloke: "You have no idea what I had to do to be able to come out golfing this weekend. I had to promise my wife that I'll paint every room in the house next weekend."

Second bloke: "That's nothing, I had to promise my wife that I'd build her a new deck for the pool."

Third bloke: "Man, you both have it easy! I had to promise my wife that I'd remodel the kitchen for her."

They continue to play the hole when they realise that the fourth bloke hasn't said a word. So they ask him, "You haven't said anything about what you had to do to be able to come golfing this weekend. What's the deal?"

The fourth bloke replies, "I just set my alarm for 5:30 am. When it goes off, I give the wife a nudge and say, 'Golf course or sex?' So she says, 'Remember to wear your sweater, dear'."

* * *

A lady is walking down the street when a particularly shabby-looking homeless woman asks her for a couple of quid. The woman takes out a fiver, and asks, "If I give you this money, will you buy some wine with it instead of dinner?"

"No. I had to stop drinking years ago," the homeless woman replies.

"Will you use it to go shopping instead of buying food?" the woman questions again.

"No, I don't waste time shopping," the homeless woman replies. "I need to spend all my time trying to stay alive."

"Will you spend this on a beauty salon instead of food?" the woman asks.

"Are you nuts?" replies the homeless woman. "I haven't had my hair done in 20 years!"

"Well," says the woman, "I'm not going to give you the money. Instead, I'm going to take you out for dinner with my husband and myself tonight."

The homeless woman is astounded. "Won't your husband be furious with you for doing that? I know I'm dirty, and I probably smell pretty disgusting."

The woman replies, "That's OK. It's important for him to see what a woman looks like after she's given up shopping, hair appointments and wine."

What do you call a woman who knows where her husband is? A widow.

* * *

A man comes home from a poker game late one night and finds his wife waiting for him with a rolling pin. "Where have you been?" she asks.

"Pack all your bags," he demands. "I lost you in a card game."

"How did you manage to do that?"

"It wasn't easy," he says. "I had to fold a royal flush."

* * *

A husband and wife visit a counsellor after 15 years of marriage.

The counsellor asks them what the problem is, and the wife starts ranting, listing every problem they've had during their marriage. She goes on and on and on; suddenly the counsellor gets up, walks around the desk and kisses her passionately. The woman shuts up immediately and sits in a daze.

The counsellor turns to the husband and says, "This is what your wife needs at least three times a week. Can you do this?"

The husband thinks for a moment and replies, "Well, I can drop her off here on Mondays and Wednesdays, but on Fridays, I'm out drinking."

* * *

Two blokes are lying in bed when one turns to the other and says, "I don't think much of this wife-swapping."

* * *

Two men's shopping trolleys collide in a supermarket.

"Sorry," says the first man. "I was looking for my wife."

The second man replies, "Me, too. Let's work together. What does yours look like?"

The first man describes his wife. "She's a tall brunette with a great figure. What about yours?"

The second man thinks for a second, "She'll turn up. Let's look for yours instead."

* * *

On the first day of university, the students are told some of the rules.

"The female dormitory is out of bounds for all male students, as is the male dormitory to the female students. Anybody caught breaking this rule will be fined £20 the first time. Anybody caught breaking this rule the second time will be fined £60. Being caught a third time will cost you £180. Are there any questions?"

A young male student pipes up, "How much for a season ticket?"

* * *

**Why do blokes get married?
So they don't have to hold their
stomachs in anymore.**

* * *

A bloke steps on one of those speak-your-weight machines that also tell your fortune.

"Listen to this," he tells his wife, showing her a small white card. "It says I'm energetic, bright, resourceful and a great lover."

"Yes," his wife nods. "And it's got your weight wrong, too!"

* * *

Two guys are trying to get in a quick eighteen holes, but there are two terrible lady golfers in front of them, hitting the ball everywhere but where it's supposed to go.

The first guy says, "Why don't you go over and ask if we can play through"

The second guy gets about halfway there and comes back, not really running but walking quite fast.

The first guy says, "What's wrong?"

His friend catches his breath then says, "One of these two women is my wife and the other one is my mistress. There is no way I could be seen with both of them! You'll have to go."

The first guy laughs, "Yes, I can see that could be a problem! You're right, I'll go over."

He gets about halfway there and comes back.

The second guy says, "What's wrong?"

"Small world," the first guy says with an apologetic grin.

* * *

This bloke's at his wedding rehearsal and decides he wants to start married life with the upper hand

He takes the vicar aside and says, "Look, I'll give you £100 if you'll change the wedding vows. When we get to the 'love, honour and obey' and 'forsaking all others, be faithful only unto her' bit, could you just leave those vows out?"

The bloke then passes the vicar the cash and walks away smugly.

The day of the wedding arrives and when it comes to the groom's vows, the vicar looks him straight in the eye and says, "Will you promise to prostrate yourself before her, obey her every command and wish, serve her breakfast in bed every morning of your life and swear eternally before God and your lovely wife that you will never even look at another women, as long as you both shall live?"

The groom gulps and looks around, then says in a tiny voice, "I will."

After the service the furious groom takes the vicar aside again and hisses, "I thought we had a deal!"

The vicar gives him back his £100 and whispers back, "She made me a much better offer."

"So tell me, what happened?" an officer asks a young lady who's just sent her husband to A&E with a broken arm.

"He talked to me," the wife replies.

"That's it? Do you happen to have a bad temper?"

"No, not at all. I'm very even-tempered."

"So why did you beat him up? Come on, you and your husband were waking up, he speaks to you and you break his arm. What did he say to you?"

"He said, 'Good morning, Lucy'"

"Is that all? And you're telling me you don't have a temper?"

"My name's Joanne," the wife replies.

* * *

A bloke is in a queue at the supermarket, when he notices that the dishy blonde behind him has raised her hand and is smiling at him.

He is rather taken aback that such a looker would be waving to him and, although she's familiar, he can't place where he knows her from, so he says, "Sorry, do you know me?"

She replies, "I may be mistaken, but I think you might be the father of one of my children."

His mind shoots back to the one and only time he has been unfaithful. "Christ!" he says. "Are you that strippergram on my stag night that I shagged on the snooker table in front of all my mates?"

"No," she replies. "I'm your son's English teacher."

A man is sitting at a bar enjoying a drink, when an exceptionally gorgeous young woman walks in. The man can't take his eyes off her. Noticing his overly attentive stare, she walks directly over to him and, before he can even apologise for gawping, she makes him an offer, "I'll do absolutely anything you want me to, no matter how kinky it is, for £100. However, there is one condition..."

Naturally, the man asks what the condition is.

"Well," says the woman, "you have to tell me what you want me to do in three words."

The man considers the proposition for a moment, takes out his wallet and slowly counts out five £20 notes. He presses each note into the young woman's hand, looks excitedly into her eyes and finally says, "Paint my house."

* * *

A man was on a blind date. He had spent the whole evening with this woman he just couldn't stand; she was everything he didn't like in a woman, so he was really bored to death. Luckily, he had prepared for just this eventuality and had asked one of his mates to call the restaurant he was eating at, just in case he needed a getaway plan. So, when the call came, he rushed over to the phone and feigned surprise and shock.

When he returned to the table, his date looked up and asked, "Is everything all right?"

He replied, "Not really. I'm afraid I'm going to have to go. My grandfather just died."

"Thank God for that," the woman said. "If yours hadn't, mine would have had to!"

* * *

One Sunday, a man is working in the garden as his wife gets up and bathes. He is clearing leaves and soon realises that he cannot find his rake, an essential tool for the job.

He can see his wife in their bedroom window, so he shouts up, "Where's my rake?"

The wife doesn't understand him and mouths, "What?"

Again the man shouts, "Where's my rake?"

The wife still doesn't understand, so shrugs her shoulders to signify a lack of comprehension. The man, tiring of shouting, points to his eye, then his knee, and then makes a raking motion with both hands. The wife is still clueless, so shrugs again, to say, "What?"

The man repeats the gestures, and mouths "eye, knee, the rake" as he does so.

The wife understands finally, and signals her reply. She points to her eye, her left breast, her bum and finally her crotch. The man's eyes nearly pop out, and it is obvious he hasn't got a clue what she is going on about. Giving up, he walks into the house and runs upstairs.

"What the hell was that all about?" he said.

The wife replies, "Eye, left tit, behind, the bush!"

MENTAL HEALTH

At one American university, students in the psychology class are attending their first lecture on emotional extremes.

"Just to establish some parameters," says the professor to a student from Arkansas, "what is the opposite of joy?"

"Sadness," replies the diligent student.

"And the opposite of depression?" he asks of a young lady from Oklahoma.

"Elation," she says.

"And you, sir," he says to a young man from Texas, "what about the opposite of woe?"

The Texan replies, "Sir, I believe that would be 'giddy up'."

* * *

A woman phoned her doctor one morning and said, "Doctor, you have to help me. My husband thinks he's a bird."

"You must send him to see me at once," said the doctor.

"I can't," said the woman. "He's flown south for the winter."

* * *

A man walks into a dentist's office and says, "I think I'm a moth."

The dentist replies, "You shouldn't be here. You should be seeing a psychiatrist."

The man replies, "I am seeing a psychiatrist."

The dentist says, "Well, then, what are you doing here?"

The man says, "Your light was on."

* * *

A university student delivers a pizza to an old man's house.

"I suppose you want a tip?" says the old man.

"That would be great," says the student, "but the other guy who does deliveries told me not to expect too much. He said if I got 50p, I'd be lucky."

The old man looks hurt. "Well, to prove him wrong, here's £5. What are you studying?"

"Applied psychology," replies the student.

* * *

A man meets a professor of psychology and asks, "Tell me, Professor, is it true there's a way to detect mental deficiency in people that appear completely normal?"

"Oh, yes," the professor answers. "All you have to do is ask them a very simple question which anybody can answer, and then monitor their replies."

"Really? Have you got an example?" the man asks, vaguely planning on fooling the professor next time he meets him.

"Take this one: Captain Cook did three trips to the Pole and died during one of them. Which one was it?"

The man laughs nervously and says, "Can you give me another example? I'm not very good at history."

A bloke goes to see a psychiatrist wearing only cling film for shorts. The shrink says, "Well, I can clearly see you're nuts."

* * *

While attending a convention, three psychiatrists take a walk.

"People are always coming to us with their guilt and fears," one says, "but we have no one to go to with our problems. Since we're all professionals, why don't we listen to each other?"

The first psychiatrist confesses, "I'm a compulsive gambler and deeply in debt, so I overcharge patients as often as I can."

The second admits, "I have a drug problem that's out of control, and I frequently pressure my patients into buying illegal drugs for me."

The third psychiatrist says, "I just can't keep a secret."

* * *

A psychology tutor is giving her class an oral test on mental health.

Singling out a student, she grills him on manic depression. "How would you diagnose a patient who walks back and forth screaming at the top of his lungs one minute, then sits in a chair weeping uncontrollably the next?"

The young man thinks for a moment, then offers his answer, "Premiership manager?"

MILITARY

A young naval student was being grilled by an old sea captain.

"What would you do if a sudden storm sprang up on the starboard?"

"Throw out an anchor, sir," the student replied.

"What would you do if another storm sprang up aft?"

"Throw out another anchor, sir."

"And if another terrific storm sprang up forward, what would you do then?" asked the captain.

"Throw out another anchor, sir."

"Hold on," said the captain, holding up his hand. "Where are you getting all these anchors from?"

"From the same place you're getting your storms, sir."

* * *

During camouflage training in a forest, a soldier is disguised as a tree. Suddenly, just as the visiting general approaches his spot, he starts shouting, lurches forward, jumps a few times up and down while spinning frantically on the spot.

"You idiot!" the officer in charge barks, quite angry at having his otherwise uneventful training disrupted right in front of the general. "Don't you know that by jumping and yelling the way you did, you could have endangered the lives of the entire company?"

"Yes sir," the solder answered apologetically, brushing away a branch from his brow. "But, if I may say so, I did stand still when a flock of pigeons used me for target practice and shat on my head. And I never moved a muscle when a large dog peed on my lower branches. But when two squirrels ran up my pants leg, and I heard the bigger say, 'Let's eat one now and save the other until winter', that did it."

During a training exercise, a commanding officer's jeep got stuck in the mud. The CO, seeing some men lounging around nearby, asked them to help him get unstuck.

"Sorry, sir," said one of the loafers, "but we've been classified dead and the umpire said we couldn't contribute in any way."

The CO turned to his driver and said, "Go and drag a couple of those dead bodies over here and throw them under the wheels to give us some traction."

* * *

Four people were travelling in the same carriage on a French train: there was an old, distinguished lady wearing a fur coat and a haughty expression; what was probably her granddaughter, a stunning 20-year-old of Playboy calibre; a highly decorated general; and a soldier fresh from boot camp.

They spent the time chatting about trivial things, and then entered a very long tunnel. While in the tunnel, the sound of a kiss was distinctly heard, followed by the unmistakable sound of a hand slapping a cheek. Silence followed, as all were lost in their respective thoughts.

The old lady was thinking, "Isn't it wonderful that, in this day and age, there are still young people ready to defend young women's honour!"

The young woman was thinking, "How strange that he would want to kiss this old hag beside me when I am available!"

The general was thinking, rubbing his stinging cheek, "I am outraged that any woman could think I would try to sneak a kiss in the dark."

The soldier had a big grin on his face and was thinking, "Isn't it great that someone can kiss the back of their own hand, then smack a general in the face and get away with it?"

* * *

A general visits the infirmary to check on his men. He goes to the first soldier, lying in his bed and asks, "What's your problem, soldier?"

"Chronic syphilis, sir."

"I see... And what treatment are you getting?"

"Five minutes with the wire brush and Dettol each day, sir."

"As it should be! And what's your ambition?"

"To get back to the front, sir."

"Good man," says the general, and he goes to the next bed. "What about you? What's your problem, soldier?"

"Chronic piles, sir"

"Nasty, that... what treatment are you getting?"

"Five minutes with the wire brush and Dettol each day, sir."

"What an efficient infirmary this is! And what's your ambition, soldier?"

"To get back to the front, sir."

"Good man," says the general, and goes to the next bed. "What's your problem, soldier?"

"Chronic gum disease, sir"

"Unusual... And what treatment are you getting?"

"Five minutes with the wire brush and disinfectant each day, sir."

"This really is a top infirmary! And what is your ambition, soldier?"

"To be treated before the other two, sir!"

During training exercises, a British Army lieutenant is driving down a muddy back road and encounters another jeep stuck in the mud with a red-faced colonel at the wheel. "Your jeep stuck, sir?" asks the lieutenant as he pulled alongside.

"Nope," replies the colonel, coming over and handing him the keys, "yours is."

* * *

Four friends in the army were doing very well indeed – so well that they decided to have a little party before the final exams. Off they went to the local whorehouse and had a wonderful time. When they woke up the following day though, they realised they had missed the examination by a few hours.

Gutted, they went to see their teacher. "Sir, we did have a little pre-exam party yesterday, but nothing much really. Only, this morning, er, the car blew a tyre. That's why we were late…," one of the friends lied glibly.

"Is that so?" asked the teacher. "That's unlucky indeed, especially since your results have been outstanding up until now."

After deliberation with his colleagues, the teacher agreed to let them take the exam in the afternoon. "The problem is that we can't get someone to keep an eye on you while you're sitting the exam, so you'll have to use four separate rooms," they were told.

Not believing their luck and amazed that their lie had actually worked, they agreed to the conditions and each entered their own examination room. The first question counted for five points and was ever so easy. Elated, sure of passing the exam, they turned the page on their exam paper to discover that the next question, counting for 95 points, asked: "Which tyre?"

MONEY

The owner of a family-run bakery was being questioned by the Inland Revenue about his tax return, having reported a net profit of £45,000 for the year.

"Why don't you people leave me alone?" the baker said. "I work like a dog, everyone in my family helps out and the place is only closed three days a year. And you want to know how I made £45,000?"

"It's not your income that bothers us," the taxman said. "It's these deductions. You listed six trips to Bermuda for you and your wife."

"Oh, that?" the owner said, smiling. "I forgot to tell you – we also deliver."

* * *

A man walks into a bank and says to the clerk, "I want to open a bloody account, you total, utter moron!"

"I'm sorry, sir?" says the clerk, taken aback.

"I said I want to open a bloody account, you dim-witted fool."

Offended by the attitude of the man, the clerk warns the customer that he doesn't have to put up with this sort of abuse and promptly leaves. Returning with the manager, he explains the situation.

"Well, sir, it seems we have a problem," says the manager.

"You're right," says the man. "I've won 50 million quid and want to open an account with you."

"I see," says the manager looking at his clerk, "so it's this idiot here that's the problem then."

* * *

A big, burly man visited the local vicar's home and asked to see the vicar's wife, a woman well known for her charity work.

"Madam," he said in a broken voice, "I wish to draw your attention to the terrible plight of a poor family in this village. The father is dead, the mother is too ill to work and the nine children are starving. They are about to be turned on to the cold, empty streets unless someone pays their rent, which amounts to £400."

"How terrible!" exclaimed the vicar's wife. "May I ask who you are?"

"I'm their landlord," he sobbed.

* * *

A man went into his bank and said to the bank teller, "I'd like to check my balance, please." "Of course," said the teller. "Can you stand on one leg on this beach ball?"

* * *

The casino is nearly empty and these two croupiers
are getting pretty bored, when a blonde turns up
at their roulette table. She flutters her eyelashes at
them and whispers breathlessly that she'd like to
have a go.

"I hope this isn't against company policy, but I
feel luckier when I'm naked," she tells the two guys.

They look around at the deserted casino and tell
her that it shouldn't be a problem. The blonde then
takes her clothes off and bets a thousand pounds
on a single roll of the ball. The roulette wheel turns
and the blonde swirls around in excitement, much
to the pleasure of the two croupiers.

"Come on, come on…!" she moans, jumping up
and down. "Yes, yes… YES! I won! I won!"

She hugs both dealers and gives them a peck on
the cheek, gathers up her clothes and her winnings
then leaves.

The two guys look at one another, grinning like
little boys.

"That was something, hey?"

"Damn right! What did she roll, anyway?"

"Hey! I thought you were watching!"

* * *

Several men are in the changing room of a golf club
when a mobile phone on a bench rings and a man
answers. He switches to hands-free and everyone
else in the room stops to listen.

"Hello," says the guy.

A female voice answers, "Honey, it's me. Are you
at the club?"

"Yes," replies the man.

"I'm at the shops now and found this beautiful
leather coat. It's only £1,000. Is it OK if I buy it?"

"Sure, go ahead if you like it that much," says the
guy, nonchalantly.

The woman goes on. "I also stopped by the
Mercedes garage and saw the new models. I saw one
I really liked."

"How much?" enquires the man.

"£60,000," says the spendthrift.

"OK, but for that price, I want it with all the
options," says the feller.

"Great!" says the woman. "Oh, and one more
thing. The house we wanted last year is back on the
market. They're asking £950,000."

"Well, then go ahead and give them an offer, but

just offer £900,000," replies the man.

"OK. I'll see you later! I love you!" the woman signs off.

"Bye, I love you, too," says the man and hangs up.

The other men in the changing room look at him in astonishment.

Then the man asks, "Anyone know whose phone this is?"

* * *

A poor man and woman were sitting on a battered sofa in their living room.
"I'm going down the pub for a bit, so put your coat on," the man said after a while.
"Oh, sweetie, are you taking me out?" the woman replied, flushing with pleasure.
"Nah, I'm turning the heat off."

A man in a bar sees a friend of his sitting and drinking by himself, looking very down.

"Hey, mate, you look terrible. What's the problem?" he asks him.

"My mother died in August," his friend replies, "and left me £25,000."

"Gee, that's tough."

"Then in September," the friend continues, "my father died, leaving me £90,000."

"Wow. Two parents gone in two months. No wonder you're depressed."

"And last month my aunt died and left me £15,000."

"Three close family members lost in three months? How sad."

"Then this month," finishes the friend, "absolutely nothing!"

* * *

A young man asked an old rich man how he made his money.

The old guy stroked his worsted wool vest and said, "Well, son, it was 1932 – the depth of the

Great Depression. I was down to my last penny, so I invested it in an apple. I spent the entire day polishing the apple and, at the end of the day, I sold it for two pence. The next morning, I invested those two pence in two apples. I spent the entire day polishing them and sold them for four pence. I continued this system for a month, by the end of which I'd accumulated a fortune of £1.35. Then my wife's father died and left us two million pounds."

* * *

Mr Smith receives a phone call from the police station.

"Mr Smith, we've apprehended the person who stole your wife's credit card. We're waiting for you to pick it up."

"Oh, let him go," Mr Smith says.

"What? You don't want to press charges?"

"Nah. Oh – and give him back the card, too. He's been spending half as much as my wife."

Four brothers grow up to become wealthy doctors and lawyers.

At a meal, they're discussing what gifts they're about to give their elderly mother for her birthday. The first brother pipes up, "I've had a big house built for her."

Another sibling chips in with, "Well, I've had a £100,000 cinema installed in that house for her."

"That's nothing," offers the third brother. "I had my car dealer deliver her a brand-new Ferrari Enzo."

The remaining brother finally speaks up. "You know how Mum loved reading the Bible, but she can't read so well these days? Well, I met this priest who has a parrot that recites the entire book! It took 12 years to teach him – and I've had to pledge to contribute £100,000 to the Church – but I've got him! Mum just has to name the chapter and verse and the parrot will recite it." The brothers are impressed.

Post-birthday, Mum pens some thank-you notes. "David, the house you built is so huge! I live in only one room, but I have to clean the whole place! Not great, but thanks anyway, son."

To her second eldest she writes, "Michael, that cinema holds 50 people... but all my friends are dead! I'll never use it. Thank you for the gesture all the same."

"Peter," she writes to her third eldest, "I'm too old to drive, so I never use the Enzo. The thought was kind. Thanks."

Finally, the youngest boy receives his letter, "Dearest Richard! You were the only son to have the good sense to put a little thought into your gift. The chicken was absolutely delicious!"

PICK AND MIX

What did the shy
little pebble want to
be when it grew up?
A little boulder!

* * *

Can a shoe box?
No, but a tin can.

* * *

**What happened to the butcher's boy
who sat on the bacon slicer?**
He got a little behind in his deliveries!

* * *

What's half
of infinity?
nity

**What do you get if you cross a lake
with a leaky boat?**
About half way and very wet!

*What word starts with "e"
and ends with "e" but only
has one letter in it?*
Envelope

**What word is always
pronounced wrong?
Wrong**

**How do you spot the most popular bloke at the
nudist colony?**
*He's the one who can have a cup of coffee in each hand
and still carry a dozen doughnuts.*

* * *

On a cold day, a man goes down to a frozen lake, cuts a hole in the ice and drops in his fishing line. He waits and waits and nothing bites. Along comes a young boy who cuts a hole in the ice, puts a worm at the end of his fishing line and has a go. After a minute or two, a large fish bites the end of his line, and the boy has to struggle to get it out of the water. This goes on for a few fish, until the frustrated man throws his fishing rod down on the ice and walks up to the boy.

"How do you do it?" he asks. "Two hours freezing my ass off without a nibble and here you come, see... twelve trout in half an hour."

"Roo Raff Too Geep Fe Rums Rom," the boy replies.

"Hey? What are you saying? Can't hear a word you say." The man shakes his head. "You'll have to speak more clearly, boy, I can't make out a word you're saying."

The boy then takes out a handful of worms from his mouth.

"You have to keep the worms warm," he enunciates clearly in an exasperated tone.

A guy was sitting alone on his train journey to London, when a couple of Norwegians entered the carriage. Sven was dressed in a smart business suit, while his friend Olf was dressed as a Teddy Boy.

After a little while, Olf stood up and went to the buffet car for a beer. He brought it back to the carriage, opened it and took a swig. He spat it out straight away, swearing loudly in Norwegian.

"What's the matter with him?" asked the guy.

"I apologise," replied Sven. "Rude Olf the Ted loathes train beer."

* * *

What's green and can kill you if it falls from a tree and lands on your head? A snooker table.

* * *

One particular Christmas season a long time ago, Santa was getting ready for his annual trip, but there were problems everywhere.

Four of his elves fell ill and the trainee elves didn't produce the toys as fast as the regular ones, so Santa was beginning to feel the pressure of being behind schedule.

Then Mrs Claus told Santa that her mum was coming to visit. This stressed Santa even more. When he went to harness the reindeer, he found that three of them were about to give birth and two had jumped the fence and escaped, heaven knows where. More stress.

Then, when he began to load the sleigh, one of the boards cracked and the toy bag fell to the ground and scattered the toys.

So, frustrated, Santa went into the house for a cup of coffee and a shot of whisky. When he went to the cupboard, he discovered that the elves had hidden the liquor and there was nothing to drink. In his frustration, he accidentally dropped the coffee pot and it broke into hundreds of little pieces all over the kitchen floor.

He went to get the broom and found that mice had eaten the straw it was made from.

Just then the doorbell rang, and Santa cursed on his way to the door. He opened the door... and there was a little angel with a great big Christmas tree.

The angel said, very cheerfully, "Merry Christmas, Santa. Isn't it just a lovely day? I have a beautiful tree for you. Isn't it just a lovely tree? Where would you like me to stick it?"

And thus began the tradition of the little angel on top of the Christmas tree.

* * *

A woman is looking at the male deodorant section in a shop. Dazzled by the sheer number of products she can buy and unable to remember what her husband usually wears, she goes to find a sales assistant.

"I need to buy some deodorant for my husband," she tells him.

"Ball or aerosol?"

"Nah, it's for under his arms."

* * *

An MP is trying his best to vote down a legal proposal by the government. He feels very frustrated and explodes, "Half of this House is made up of cowards, and the other half is corrupt!"

He is instantly booed by his colleagues and threatened with being barred and losing his office if he doesn't apologise right away.

"OK," he says. "Half of this House is not made of cowards and the other half is not corrupt."

* * *

One day, the Lone Ranger and his faithful friend Tonto were surrounded by hostile Indians. Negotiations had fallen through and the horde was ready to attack. The Lone Ranger turned to Tonto and said, "My dear friend, what do we do?" "What do you mean, what do we do, white man?" Tonto asked.

After having dug through soil for a month, British scientists discovered copper wire dating back 500 years, buried deep. They came to the conclusion that the British people already had a telephone exchange 500 years ago. Not to be outdone, the Americans started digging too, and claimed they had found, buried at a depth of 600 metres, a network of fibre optic wire dating back 2,000 years which proved the American people had the Internet at the time Jesus was born. The Belgian government decided to have a go too. Their team of scientists dug and dug, but found nothing. The Belgian government therefore stated that the results of this experiment clearly showed that 2,000 years ago Belgians had mobile phones.

* * *

A guy sticks his head round the door of the barber's shop and asks, "How long before I can get a haircut?"

The barber looks around the shop and replies, "About two hours."

The guy leaves and doesn't come back. A few days

later, the same guy sticks his head round the door and asks, "How long before I can get a haircut?"

The barber looks around the shop full of customers and says, "About two hours."

The guy leaves and doesn't come back.

A week later, the same guy sticks his head in the shop and asks, "How long before I can get a haircut?"

The barber looks around the shop and replies, "About an hour and a half."

The guy leaves.

The barber looks over at a friend in the shop and says, "Hey, Bill. Follow that guy and see where he goes." In a little while, Bill comes back into the shop laughing hysterically.

"So where did he go when he left here?"

Bill grins and says, "To your house."

* * *

Why are pirates called pirates?
They just arrrr!

* * *

Two MPs are talking late at night in the House of Commons bar.

"How do you choose the right person to back for Prime Minister?" says the younger politician.

"Easy," says the old buffer. "Just adopt the same procedure as you would when choosing a taxi driver."

"What's that?" says the young MP.

"Just decide which one will cost you least and not get you killed."

* * *

A redneck, named Kenny, buys a donkey from a farmer for $100. The farmer agrees to deliver the donkey the next day.

The next day the farmer drives up and says, "Sorry, son, but I have some bad news; the donkey's dead."

Kenny replies, "Well, then, just give me my money back."

The farmer says, "I can't do that. I went and spent it already."

Kenny says, "OK, then, just bring me the dead donkey."

The farmer asks, "What are you going to do with him?"

Kenny says, "I'm going to raffle him off."

A month later, the farmer meets up with Kenny and asks, "What happened with that dead donkey?"

Kenny says, "I raffled him off, like I said I was going to. I sold 500 tickets at two dollars apiece and made a profit of $998."

The farmer says, "Didn't anyone complain?"

Kenny says, "Just the guy who won. So I gave him his two dollars back."

* * *

Every morning a man took the ferry to work. One morning, he woke up and found he had no electricity. He had no idea what time it was, but assumed he was late since he had a tendency to sleep late anyway.

So he scoffed down his breakfast, rushed to the port where he saw the ferry ten feet from the dock, and took a running leap. He barely made it, skidding across the deck of the boat, and hurting himself quite badly.

"You know," said the captain, "in another minute we would have docked."

* * *

One day, a French spy received a coded message from a British MI6 agent. It read: S370HSSV-0773H.

The spy was stumped, so he sent it to his similarly clueless boss, who forwarded it to Russia. The Russians couldn't solve it either, so they asked the Germans. The Germans, having received this same message during WWII from the Brits, suggested turning it upside down.

An artist asks a gallery owner if there's been any interest in his paintings recently. "I have good news and bad news," the gallery owner tells him. "The good news is a gentleman enquired about your work and wondered if it would appreciate in value after your death. When I told him it would, he bought all 15 of your paintings."

"That's great," the artist says. "What's the bad news?"

"He was your doctor."

* * *

The Hunchback of Notre Dame returns home from a hard day ringing the cathedral bells, and finds his beautiful wife standing in the kitchen holding a wok.

"Fantastic, Esmeralda," says the Hunchback, "I really fancy some Chinese food."

"Oh, no, not tonight, Quasi," she says, "I'm ironing your shirts."

Late one night, a young chap was walking home from a club. Most of the streetlights in the area were broken. Suddenly, he heard a strange noise. Startled, he turned and saw a coffin following him. He started to jog, but he heard the coffin speed up behind him. Eventually, he made it to his front door, but he knew the coffin was only seconds behind. He dived inside, slamming the front door. Suddenly, there was a crash as the coffin smashed its way through the front door. In horror, the young lad fled upstairs to the bathroom and locked the door.

With an almighty smash, the bathroom door flew off its hinges and the coffin stood in its place. Desperate, the young man reached into his bathroom cabinet. He grabbed a bar of Imperial Leather soap and threw it at the coffin, but still it came. He grabbed a can of Lynx deodorant and threw it, but still it came.

Finally, he threw some cough mixture. The coffin stopped.

* * *

As Claude the hypnotist took to the stage, he announced, "Unlike most stage hypnotists, I intend to hypnotise each and every member of the audience."

Claude then withdrew a beautiful antique pocket watch from his coat. "I want you each to keep your eye on this antique watch. It's a very special watch. It has been in my family for six generations."

He began to swing the watch gently back and forth while quietly chanting, "Watch the watch. Watch the watch. Watch the watch. Watch the watch. Watch the watch..."

Hundreds of pairs of eyes followed the swaying watch – until, unexpectedly, it slipped from Claude's fingers and fell to the floor, breaking into a hundred pieces.

"Sh*t!" exclaimed the hypnotist, loudly.

It took three weeks to clean the seats.

* * *

Jack and Bob are driving when they get caught in a blizzard. They pull into a nearby farmhouse and ask the attractive lady of the house if they can spend the night.

"I'm recently widowed," she explains, "and I'm afraid the neighbours will talk if I let you stay here."

"Not to worry," Jack says. "We'll be happy to sleep in the barn."

Nine months later, Jack gets a letter from the widow's attorney. After reading it, he quickly drives around to Bob's house.

"Bob, remember that good-looking widow at the farm we stayed at?"

"Yes, I remember her," says Bob.

"Did you happen to get up in the middle of the night, go up to the house and have sex with her?" asks Jack.

"Yes, I have to admit that I did," replies Bob. "Did you happen to use my name instead of telling her your name?" asks Jack.

Embarrassed, Bob says, "Yeah, I'm afraid I did."

"Well, thanks a lot, pal," says Jack. "She just died and left me her farm!"

* * *

A cowboy walks into a saloon and says, "Who painted my horse's balls yellow?"

Suddenly, a huge, mean-looking cowboy stands up and says, "I did."

So the first guy looks up at him and says, "I just wanted to let you know the first coat's dry."

* * *

The flower vendor is an old hand at unloading his last few bunches each day. Appealing to a businessman on his way home, the vendor says, "How about a nice bunch of roses to surprise your wife?"

"Haven't got a wife," the businessman responds.

"Then how about some carnations for your girlfriend?" the vendor proposes without missing a beat.

"Haven't got a girlfriend."

The vendor breaks into a big smile. "Oh, then you'll want all the flowers I've got left. You have a lot to celebrate!"

* * *

"Knock, knock."

"Who's there?"

"Control freak. Now this is where you say, 'Control freak who?'"

* * *

Why should you never replace your sandwich toaster?

Better the Breville you know.

* * *

A man goes to his local gym to ask about yoga classes for beginners.

The instructor asks, "How flexible are you?"

"Well," replies the man, "I can't do Wednesdays."

* * *

Why do bagpipers walk when they play?
To get away from the sound.

* * *

A man has huge feet. Wherever he goes, people take the mick. Sitting on the beach wall with his plates dangling in the water, a vicar strolls past and can see the man is upset, so he walks over and asks, "What's the matter?"

"I'm so depressed," replies the man. "Everywhere I go, people ridicule me for the size of my feet."

The vicar comes up with a plan and tells the man, "Dye your hair a brilliant green and, that way, people will look at your hair and not your feet!"

The man thanks the vicar for the advice, goes to the nearest hair salon and has his hair dyed. He walks out feeling fantastic – better than he's felt in a long time. He bounds down the road and a passer-by shouts out, "Hey, you with the green hair!"

He turns around and shouts confidently back, "Yeah?"

"Ha, ha," laughs the passer-by. "You've got bloody massive feet, mate!"

An accordionist is driving home from a late-night gig. Feeling tired, he pulls into a service station for some coffee. While waiting to pay, he remembers that he locked his car doors but left the accordion in plain view on the back seat of his car! He rushes out only to realise that he is too late. The back window of his car has been smashed and somebody's already thrown in two more accordions.

* * *

There are two grains of sand in the desert. One turns to the other and says, "Busy here, isn't it?"

* * *

Did you hear about the man who fell into the machine at the upholsterer's factory? He's fully recovered.

* * *

A redneck is walking down the road and sees his cousin coming toward him with a sack.

"What you got there?" he asks.

"Some chickens," replies his equally slack-jawed cousin.

"If I can guess how many you got, can I have one?"

"Shoot. If you guess right, I'll give you both of 'em."

"OK... five."

* * *

A man walks into a record shop and asks, "What have you got by The Doors?" The owner replies, "A mop and a fire extinguisher."

* * *

A guy goes into a girl's house, and she shows him into the living room. She excuses herself to go to the kitchen to make some drinks. As he's standing there alone, he notices a vase on the mantelpiece. He picks it up and, as he's looking at it, she walks back in.

He says, "What's this?"

"Oh, my father's ashes are in there," she replies.

Turning red, he apologizes.

She continues, "Yeah, he's too lazy to go to get an ashtray."

* * *

A large cup and two smaller ones go out for a meal at a posh restaurant. When the bill arrives, the small cups do a runner, leaving their pal to pay up.

A week later, the three are back and, once again, the large cup is left behind to settle the bill.

The waiter comes up to him, and says, "No offence, mate, but I think your two pals are taking you for a mug."

* * *

A man goes to a barbershop for a shave. While the barber is lathering him up, he mentions the problems he has getting a close shave around the cheeks.

"I have just the thing," says the barber, taking a small wooden ball from a nearby drawer. "Just place this between your cheek and gum."

The man places the ball in his mouth and the barber proceeds with the closest shave the man has ever experienced.

After a few strokes, the client asks in garbled speech, "But what if I swallow it?"

"No problem," says the barber. "Just bring it back tomorrow like everyone else does."

* * *

A man bought a new fridge for his house. To get rid
of his old fridge, he put it in the driveway and hung
a sign on it which read: "Free to good home. You
want it, you take it."

For three days, the fridge sat there without
even one person looking twice at it. He eventually
decided that people were too suspicious. It looked
too good to be true.

He changed the sign to read: "Fridge for sale,
£50."

The next day someone stole it.

* * *

There was a young man who wanted to become a
great writer.

When asked to define 'great', he said,
"I want to write stuff that people will react to on
a truly emotional level – stuff that will make them
cry and howl in pain
and anger!"

He now works for Microsoft, writing error
messages.

* * *

The CIA had an opening for an assassin. After all the interviews and tests, three candidates were left – two men and a woman. For the final test, CIA agents took one man to a door and gave him a gun. "We must know that you'll follow instructions, no matter what. Inside this room is your wife. Kill her."

The man said, "I could never do that."

The agent said, "Then you're not the man for this job."

The same thing happened with the second man. Finally, the woman is given the same instructions to kill her husband. She took the gun and went into the room. Shots were heard. Then screaming and banging on the walls. Then silence. Then the woman comes out, wiping sweat from her brow.

"This gun was loaded with blanks," she said. "I had to beat him to death with the chair."

An efficiency expert concludes his lecture with a note of caution.

"You need to be careful about trying these techniques at home," he says.

"Why?" asks a man in the audience.

"I watched my wife's routine at breakfast for years," the expert explains. "She made lots of trips between the fridge, cooker, table and cabinets, often carrying a single item at a time. One day I told her, 'Honey, why don't you try carrying several things at once?'"

"Did it save time?" the guy in the audience asked.

"Actually, yes," replies the expert. "It used to take her 30 minutes to make breakfast. Now I do it in ten."

* * *

A little old lady answered a knock on the door one day, only to be confronted by a well-dressed young man carrying a vacuum cleaner.

"Good morning," said the young man. "If I could take a couple minutes of your time, I would like to demonstrate the very latest in high-powered vacuum cleaners."

"Get lost!" said the old lady. "I haven't got any money," and she proceeded to close the door.

Quick as a flash, the young man wedged his foot in the door and pushed it wide open.

"Don't be too hasty!" he said. "Not until you have at least seen my demonstration." With that, he slung a bucket of horse crap all over her hallway carpet. "If this vacuum cleaner does not remove all traces of this from your carpet, madam, I will personally eat the remainder."

"Well," she said, "I hope you've got a bloody good appetite, because the electricity was cut off this morning."

* * *

Customer: I'd like a pair of stockings for my wife.
Storekeeper: Sheer?
Customer: No, she's at home.

POLICE AND CRIMINALS

A policeman in a small town stopped a motorist who was speeding down the High Street. "But, officer," the man began, "I can explain."

"Quiet!" snapped the officer. "I'm going to let you spend the night in jail until the sergeant gets back."

"But, officer, I just wanted to say..."

"I said be quiet! You're going to jail!"

A few hours later the officer looked in on his prisoner and said, "Lucky for you, the sarge is at his daughter's wedding so he'll be in a good mood when he gets back."

"Don't count on it," answered the bloke in the cell. "I'm the groom."

A couple are walking down the street when the girl stops in front of a jewellery store and says, "Darling, look at that necklace! It's so beautiful."

"No problem," replies her bloke as he throws a brick through the window and grabs the sparkler.

A little later the girl points to a bracelet in the window of another shop.

"Ooh," she says, "I'd love that too!"

"No problem," says her boyfriend and, again, throws a brick through the window.

A little later they pass yet another shop when she sees a diamond ring. "Oh, honey, isn't that lovely?" she says.

"Hang about!" he says. "What do you think I am? Made of bricks?"

* * *

Thieves broke into the police station and stole the only toilet.
The police had nothing to go on.

* * *

A policeman pulls over a car for swerving and asks the driver to take a breathalyser test.

"I can't do that," says the man. "I'm an asthmatic. The breathalyser could bring on an attack."

So the policeman suggests a urine sample.

"Can't do it," says the man. "I'm a diabetic, so my urine always has strange stuff in it."

"Well," says the angry policeman, "why don't you just get out of the car and walk along this white line?"

"Sorry," says the man, "but I can't do that either."

"Why not?" asks the officer.

"Because I'm drunk."

* * *

A mafia godfather finds out that his bookkeeper has swindled him out of ten million dollars. This bookkeeper is deaf, so the godfather brings along his attorney, who knows sign language.

The godfather asks the bookkeeper, "Where's the ten million you embezzled from me?"

The attorney, using sign language, asks the bookkeeper where the money is hidden.

The bookkeeper signs, "I don't know what you're talking about."

The attorney tells the godfather, "He says he doesn't know what you're talking about."

At this point, the godfather pulls out a 9mm pistol, puts it to the bookkeeper's temple, cocks it and says, "Ask him again!"

"He'll kill you if you don't talk," signs the attorney.

The bookkeeper signs back, "OK. You win! The money is buried in my cousin Enzo's back yard."

The godfather asks the attorney, "Well, what'd he say?"

The attorney replies, "He says you wouldn't dare..."

* * *

The cops are ordered to clean up the High Street for a big parade, and are patrolling the pavements when a drunk staggers towards them.

"Excuse me, offisher," he says to one constable, "could you pleash tell me the time?"

The constable frowns at him. "One o'clock," he says, before whacking him once over the head with his truncheon.

"Christ!" says the drunk, reeling. "I'm glad I didn't ask you an hour ago!"

* * *

A policeman got out of his car and the lad who was stopped for speeding rolled down his window. "I've been waiting for you all day," the policeman said. "Yeah," replied the lad. "Well, I got here as fast as I could."

* * *

A policeman was interrogating three men who were training to become detectives. To test their skills in recognising a suspect, he shows the first man a picture for five seconds and then hides it.

"This is your suspect. How would you recognise him?"

The first man answers, "That's easy, we'll catch him fast because he only has one eye!"

The policeman says, "Well… uh… that's because the picture shows his profile."

Slightly flustered by this ridiculous response, he flashes the picture for five seconds at the second man and asks, "This is your suspect. How would you recognise him?"

The second man says, "That shouldn't be too difficult, he only has one ear!"

The policeman angrily responds, "What's the matter with you two? Of course only one eye and one ear are showing – it's a picture of his profile! Is that the best answer you can come up with?"

Extremely frustrated at this point, he shows the picture to the third man and in a very testy voice asks, "This is your suspect. How would you recognise him?" He quickly adds, "Think hard before giving me a stupid answer."

The third man looks at the picture intently for a moment and says, "The suspect wears contact lenses."

The policeman is surprised and speechless, because he really doesn't know himself whether the suspect wears contacts or not. "Well, that's an interesting answer...wait here for a few minutes while I check his file, and I'll get back to you on that."

He leaves the room and goes to his office, checks the suspect's file in his computer and comes back with a beaming smile on his face. "Wow! I can't believe it... you're right! The suspect does in fact wear contact lenses. How were you able to make such an astute observation?"

"That's easy," the third man replied. "He can't wear glasses because he only has one eye and one ear."

* * *

It's 2am and the police stop a man in the street and ask for ID.

"So, what are you doing in the streets at such an hour?" one of the policemen asks while his colleague reads the guy's ID.

"I'm back from giving a lecture," he replies. "I'm a lecturer."

"Ha! Pull the other one. You don't look like a lecturer to me!"

His colleague taps him on the shoulder and whispers that his ID says that he is, indeed, a lecturer.

"So what? Who were you giving a lecture to at this time of night anyway" the policeman asks triumphantly.

"My wife."

* * *

Two burglars have broken into a pharmacy and managed to steal a large quantity of the drug Viagra. The local police are now on the look-out for two hardened criminals.

* * *

A police patrol stops a car at random in a big city. They inspect the car and, to their surprise, find an impressive collection of knives in the boot.

"What are you doing with all these knives?" the officer asks, while the other cop takes his truncheon out of his holster.

"You don't understand," the driver says. "I'm an artist, a juggler. I work in a circus. These are my stage knives."

"Pull the other one."

"Seriously, officer. Let me give a demonstration."

The officer is inclined to refuse the request but, then again, he's got back-up, so he hands a couple of knives to the guy.

The driver picks them up and shows the policemen that the knives aren't sharp, and then he starts juggling. When it is quite evident that he's not going to harm anyone, the officer lets him juggle with a couple more.

Just at this moment, another car passes by. The driver looks at his wife and says in awed tones, "Oh, my God! They're really getting tough with alcohol testing now! Look at what they're asking people to do!"

* * *

"Good morning, officer," a guy says to the policeman behind the desk at the station. "It's about the guy who broke into my house last night."

"Yes, how can I help you?"

"Well, I was wondering if I could have a chat with him."

"I'm sorry, sir. We can't allow that," the policeman replies. "You'll get plenty of chances to state your case during the court hearing."

"Oh, you don't understand," the guy insists. "I don't want to insult him or anything, quite the contrary. You see, he managed to get into our house last night without waking up the wife. I've been trying to do exactly that for the past ten years, so I'd like to know how he did it."

* * *

A prisoner receives a letter from his wife. She writes to him about this and that and concludes with a gardening question, "I remember how you loved to work in the garden, so here's a question for you. I bought some lettuce plants I'd like to plant in the back garden. When is a good time?"

The prisoner doesn't answer straight away, because he knows that all the mail is read by the staff before being given to the prisoner. So he thinks about it for a couple of days, then sends the following message to his wife, "Honey, you can't plant them in the back garden! Please, don't touch the back garden! I left something there which I want to pick up when I get out of this place."

A week later, he receives another letter from his wife which concludes, "By the way, I didn't touch the back garden, as you told me. Unfortunately, a bunch of policemen turned up the other day and dug it all up."

To which the prisoner replies, "Now is the right time to plant the lettuce."

An escaped convict breaks into a house, and the young couple living there end up tied to the bed, helpless.

Whispering in his wife's ear, the husband says, "Honey, I know this is a lot to ask, but there's a chance that this is the guy they had a picture of on TV. He's a murderer and he's been in jail for years. He might not have had sex for ages. If he attempts anything, we'll have to be brave. It's the only chance we've got to stay alive."

The wife nods and replies, "I'm so glad you are taking it this way. I just heard him say you look cute in your satin pyjama bottoms."

* * *

Two men are robbing a hotel.
"I hear sirens. Jump!" says the first one.
"But we're on the 13th floor!" his fellow-thief replies.
"This is no time to be superstitious!"

284

* * *

The latest police advertising campaign has attracted very few potential recruits. The force needs men, though, so the entrance examination has to be made easier and Sergeant Smith ends up interviewing John, who doesn't look like policeman material at all. Nonetheless, equal opportunity and all that.

Sergeant Smith asks the first question. "Right, back to basics," he says in a bored tone. "Numeracy. What's one plus one?"

John replies, "11".

The sergeant's eyebrows shoot up. It's not the answer he was looking for but, in a way, it's not an incorrect answer either.

"OK. Literacy next. Give me two days in the week that start with the letter T."

"Today and tomorrow," John replies proudly.

Sergeant Smith is aghast. Once again, this guy has kind of answered right, while giving an utterly different answer to what was expected. Knowing that policemen are often asked to think outside the box, he reasons that this John person might prove handy after all.

"I see. General knowledge. Who killed John F Kennedy?"

John is silent. After a minute or so, his eyes downcast, he replies, "I don't know."

"No big deal," Sergeant Smith says. "Come back to me when you do know."

"Sure thing. I'll work on it," replies John. He nods smartly to the sergeant and leaves.

"So, how did the interview go?" his wife asks.

"Pretty good," John says. "Only one day at the office and I'm already on a murder case."

* * *

A rookie is anxious to assert his authority. He is patrolling the streets, eagle-eyed, in the company of an old veteran, when they receive a call asking them to disperse a small crowd which is causing trouble near a pub.

They drive there and, sure enough, there is a small crowd on the pavement. His colleague stops the car. The rookie gets out and walks towards the crowd with a very macho gait.

"The fun's over, citizens. Time to go back home now," he says gruffly. No one moves.

"I said to go back home now people. We don't want any trouble, do we?" he threatens. Slowly, reluctantly, they start shuffling off.

Satisfied, he goes back to the car and asks his more experienced colleague who's been waiting for him, "So, how did I do?"

"Not bad," he replied with a chuckle. "Not bad at all, considering that this is a bus stop."

* * *

Three criminals are running away from the cops, when they providentially stumble upon an old barn to hide in. They find three big sacks on the floor of the barn and promptly jump in them. About a minute later, a police car comes to a screaming halt by the barn door and a policeman steps out. He enters the barn and spots the suspicious-looking sacks. He kicks the first one.

"Meow," says the first criminal.

"It must be a cat," says the policeman, and he kicks the second sack.

"Woof," says the second criminal.

"Must be a dog," mutters the policeman, and he

kicks the third sack.

"Potatoes," says the third criminal.

* * *

Upon arriving home after work, a woman discovers that she's been burgled. She throws herself on the sofa, mourning the loss of her stuff for a while, then calls the police. A few minutes later, a policeman knocks on her door, holding a dog on a leash in the hope of catching any scent of the burglars.

The woman stares at the pair, then collapses on the sofa again and moans, "Just my luck! I get burgled, and they send me a blind policeman!"

* * *

A man is talking in his favourite bar with his favourite friends on a Sunday night.

"So, check this out – last night when I was down here with you lot, a bloody burglar broke into my house."

"Well out of order," says his mate.

"Did he get anything?" says another.

"Yup," says the man, "a smack in the face, a kick up the backside, a plank between the legs and a dinner-plate over his head – the missus thought it was me coming home pissed again!"

* * *

On his first night in prison, a convict is glumly eating his dinner when another inmate jumps to his feet, shouts, "Thirty-seven!" and all the other inmates laugh hysterically.

Another shouts back, "Four hundred and twenty!" and gets the same reaction.

"What's going on?" says the new inmate to his cellmate.

"It's like this," says the convict. "We only have one joke book in this prison, and everyone knows all the jokes off by heart, so instead of telling the whole joke, we just stand up and shout out a page number."

A few days later, the new convict decides that it's time to join in, so he stands up and shouts, "Fourteen!"

Total silence ensues. Turning to his cellmate, he asks, "What went wrong?"

The convict replies, "It's the way you tell 'em."

The usher of a theatre notices a guy sprawled across three seats in the front row. The theatre isn't full, but this is no reason why this guy should feel entitled to act this way, so the usher goes to him and whispers, "Sir, could you please sit properly?"

There is no answer. The guy refuses to budge. Irritated, the usher repeats his sentence, to no avail. He decides to fetch the manager.

The manager arrives a few minutes later and orders the guy to sit up properly. There's no answer, and the guy refuses to move. "I'm warning you, sir. If you don't behave in a civil manner, I'll have to call the police."

All he gets for his pains is a wall of silence, so he decides to carry out his threat and he calls the police. A policeman turns up and walks to the spot where this guy is sprawled across three seats in a most anti-social manner.

"OK, sir, please be reasonable and sit up properly. You're disrupting the show."

As there's no answer, he sighs and opens his notebook with exaggerated drama.

"Don't force me to do this, sir," he warns. "If you

don't behave properly, I'll have to take you to the station." As the guy remains silent, the policeman shrugs and takes the top off his ballpoint pen.

"All right, then. What's your name?" No answer.

"Stubborn to the last, I see," the policeman chides. "OK, maybe you don't understand me. Maybe you're not a British citizen." Slowly and distinctly, he asks, "Where do you come from?"

The shape on the seat finally manages to feebly lift his head, and croaks, "The balcony…"

RELIGION

*Two Bishops were
tucked up in bed.
Which one was
wearing a nightie?
Mrs Bishop.*

* * *

A priest and vicar from the local parishes are standing by the side of the road holding up a sign that reads, "The end is near! Turn yourself around now before it's too late!"

They plan to hold up the sign to each passing car.

"Leave us alone, you religious nuts!" yells the first driver as he speeds by.

Seconds later the men of God hear screeching tyres and a big splash from around the corner.

"Do you think," says one clergyman to the other, "we should just put up a sign that says 'Bridge Out' instead?"

* * *

After Quasimodo's death, the bishop of the cathedral of Notre Dame sent word through the streets of Paris that a new bell ringer was needed. The bishop decided that he would conduct the interviews personally, and went up into the belfry to begin the screening process. After observing several applicants demonstrate their skills, he was going to call it a day when an armless man approached him and announced that he was here to apply.

The bishop was incredulous. "You have no arms!"

"No matter," said the man, "Observe!"

He then began striking the bells with his face, producing a beautiful melody on the carillon. The bishop listened in astonishment, convinced that he had finally found a suitable replacement for Quasimodo. Suddenly, rushing forward to strike a bell, the armless man tripped and plunged headlong out of the belfry window, falling to his death in the street below. The stunned bishop rushed down to get to his side. When he reached to street, a crowd had gathered around the fallen figure, drawn by the beautiful music they had heard moments before.

As they silently parted to let the bishop through,

one of them asked, "Bishop, who was this man?"

"I don't know his name," the bishop sadly replied, "but his face rings a bell."

* * *

The following day, despite the sadness that weighed heavily on his heart due to the unfortunate death of the armless campanologist, the bishop continued his interviews for the bell ringer of Notre Dame.

The first man to approach him said, "Your Excellency, I am the brother of the poor, armless wretch who fell to his death from this very belfry yesterday. I pray that you honour his life by allowing me to replace him in this duty."

The bishop agreed to give the man an audition. As the armless man's brother stooped to pick up a mallet to strike the first bell, he groaned, clutched at his chest and died on the spot. Two monks, hearing the bishop's cries of grief at this second tragedy, rushed up the stairs to his side. "What has happened?" the first asked breathlessly. "Who is this man?"

"I don't know his name," sighed the distraught bishop, "but he's a dead ringer for his brother."

After his business goes bust, a redneck called Scooter finds himself in dire financial trouble and resorts to prayer.

"God, please help me," he wails. "I've lost my business, and if I don't get some money, I'm going to lose my car as well. Please let me win the lottery."

Saturday night comes, and Scooter watches aghast as someone else wins. Again, he begins to pray. "God, please let me win the lottery! I've lost my business, my car, and I'm going to lose my house."

Next Saturday night comes, and Scooter still has no luck. Once again, he prays.

"God, why haven't you helped me?" he cries. "I've lost my business, my house, my car, and my children are starving! I've always been a good servant to you; please let me win the lottery just this once!"

Suddenly, there is a blinding flash of light as the heavens open, and Scooter is confronted with the glowing, ethereal vision of God himself.

"Scooter," he booms. "Meet me halfway on this. Buy a ticket."

* * *

A nun, badly needing to use the toilet, walks into a local club.

The place is hopping with music and loud conversation and every once in a while, the lights turn off. Each time this happens, the place erupts into cheers. However, when the revellers spy the nun, the room goes dead silent.

"May I please use the ladies'?" the nun asks.

The bartender replies, "Sure, but I should warn you that there's a statue of a naked man in there wearing only a fig leaf."

"Well, in that case I'll just look the other way," says the nun.

After a few minutes the nun reappears, and the whole place stops long enough to give the nun a loud round of applause.

The nun walks over to the bartender and says, "I don't understand. Why did they applaud me just because I went to the ladies'?"

"You see," laughs the bartender, "every time that fig leaf on the statue is lifted up, the lights go out."

* * *

A priest walks into a pet shop to buy a bird.
The owner beckons him over to a parrot.
"This is a special parrot," he says. "If you
pull the string on the left leg, he recites
'The Lord's Prayer'. Pull the string on his
right leg, and he recites Genesis."
"What if you pull both strings?" asks the
priest.
The parrot screams, "Then I fall off my
perch, you idiot!"

* * *

An old woman is on a plane and is getting
increasingly worried about the turbulence around
her. She turns to the vicar next to her and asks:
"Reverend, you are a man of God. Why can't you
do something about this problem?"

"Lady," says the vicar. "I'm in sales, not
management."

An American decided to write a book about famous churches around the world. For his first chapter, he decided to write about famous English and Scottish cathedrals. So he bought a plane ticket and made the trip to London, thinking that he would work his way northwards.

On his first day, he was inside a church taking photographs when he noticed a golden telephone mounted on the wall with a sign that read '£10,000 per call'. The American, being intrigued, asked a priest who was strolling by what the telephone was used for. The priest replied that it was a direct line to heaven and that for £10,000, you could talk to God.

The American thanked the priest and went along his way. Next stop was in Salisbury. There, at a very large cathedral, he saw the same golden telephone with the same sign under it. He wondered if this was the same kind of telephone he saw in London, so he asked a nearby nun what its purpose was. She told him that it was a direct line to heaven and that for £10,000 he could talk to God.

"OK, thank you," said the American.

He then travelled to Bath, Coventry, York and Newcastle and in every church, he saw the same golden telephone with the same '£10,000 per call' sign under it. With his book going well, he left England and travelled north to Scotland. Again, at his first stop at St. Giles Cathedral in Edinburgh, there was the same golden telephone, but this time the sign under it read '10p per call'.

The American was surprised, so he asked the minister about the sign.

"Vicar, I've travelled all over England, and I've seen this same golden telephone in many cathedrals and churches. I'm told that it is a direct line to heaven, but in all the cities in England the price was £10,000 per call. Why is it so cheap here?"

The minister smiled and answered, "You're in Scotland now, my child. It's a local call."

* * *

A middle-aged woman has a heart attack and is taken to the hospital. While on the operating table, she has a near-death experience.

Seeing God, she asks, "Is my time up?"

God says, "No, you have another 43 years, two months and eight days to live."

Upon recovery, the woman decides to stay in the hospital and have a facelift, liposuction and a tummy tuck.

While crossing the street on her way home, she's killed by an ambulance. Arriving in front of God, she demands, "I thought you said I had another 40 years?"

God replies, "I didn't recognise you."

* * *

What's black and white and tells the Pope to get lost? A nun who's just won the lottery.

* * *

A drunk is stumbling through the woods when
he comes across a preacher baptising people in the
river. He trips and falls before the holy man.

Almost overcome by the smell of alcohol, the
preacher pipes up, "Lord have mercy on your
drunken soul, brother. Are you ready to find Jesus?"

Out of his skull, the drunk agrees, "Yes, I am!"

And with that, the preacher grabs him and dunks
him under the water. Moments later, he drags the
boozer back up, "Brother, have you found Jesus?"

"No, preacher," stammers the drunk, "I haven't"

Stunned by this, the preacher sends the drunk
down again... this time leaving him a little longer.

Finally, he drags him back up again. "Rid your
soul of the poison, brother. Have you found Jesus?"

Gasping for air, the drunk splutters a reply, "No,
preacher, I have not!"

At his wits' end, the preacher sends the drunk
down one last time. A full minute later, he pulls
him out. "For the love of God," shouts the preacher,
"tell me you've found Jesus!"

Coughing his lungs up, the drunk wipes his eyes

and turns to the preacher, "You sure this is where he fell in?"

A man was walking down the street in a sweat, because he had an important meeting and couldn't find a parking space.

Looking up towards heaven he said, "Lord, take pity on me. If you can find me a parking space, I'll go to church every Sunday for the rest of my life and give up lager." Miraculously, a parking space appeared.

The man looked up to heaven again and said, "Never mind – I found one."

* * *

God is sitting in heaven when a scientist says to him, "Lord, we don't need you any more. Science has finally figured out a way to create life out of nothing. We can now do what you did in the beginning."

"Oh, is that so? Tell me," replies God.

"Well," says the scientist, "we can take dirt and breathe life into it, thus creating man."

"Well, that's interesting. Show me," booms God.

So the scientist bends down to the earth and starts to breathe on the soil.

"Oi!" says God. "Get your own dirt."

* * *

What do you get when you mix a laxative with holy water? A religious movement.

* * *

A minister is winding up his sermon one Sunday in church.

"Next Sunday I am going to preach on the subject of liars and, as a preparation for my discourse, I would like you all to read the seventeenth chapter of Mark," he says.

On the following Sunday, the vicar walks to the front of the church and says, "Now then. Those of you who have done as I requested and read the seventeenth chapter of Mark, please raise your hands."

Nearly every hand in the congregation shoots up.

The vicar looks stern and says, "You are the ones I want to talk to about lying. There is no seventeenth chapter of Mark."

* * *

Jesus and Satan are having an ongoing argument about who's better on their computer. Finally, God says, "I am going to set up a test which will take two hours, and I will judge who does the better job."

So Satan and Jesus sit down at the keyboards and type away.

They do everything their PCs can handle. But, ten minutes before the time's up, lightning suddenly flashes across the sky, and the electricity goes off.

Satan stares at his blank screen and screams every curse word known in the underworld. Jesus just sighs. The electricity finally flickers back on, and each of them reboots.

Satan starts searching, frantically screaming, "It's gone! It's all gone! I lost everything when the power went out!"

Meanwhile, Jesus quietly starts printing out all his files from the past two hours. Satan sees this and becomes even more irate. "Wait! He cheated! How did he do it!?"

God shrugs and says, "Jesus saves."

* * *

A priest is preparing a man for his passing over. Whispering firmly, the priest says, "Denounce the devil! Let him know how little you think of him!"

The dying man says nothing. The priest repeats his order.

Still the man says nothing.

The priest asks, "Why do you refuse to denounce the devil and his evil?"

The dying man replies, "Until I know for sure where I'm headed, I don't think I ought to aggravate anybody."

* * *

A drunken priest is pulled over for speeding. Smelling alcohol on the father's breath and noticing a wine bottle on the passenger seat, the copper asks, "Sir, have you been drinking?"

The minister replies, "Just water."

"Then tell me," the policeman enquires.

"How is it that I can smell wine?"

The minister looks down at the bottle and exclaims, "Good Lord, He's done it again!"

* * *

An atheist explorer in the deepest Amazon suddenly finds himself surrounded by a group of bloodthirsty natives. Upon surveying the situation, he says quietly to himself, "Oh, God. I'm screwed this time!"

There is a ray of light from heaven and a voice booms out, "No, you are not screwed. All you have to do is pick up that stone at your feet and bash in the head of the chief standing in front of you."

So the explorer picks up the stone and proceeds to bash the chief until he's unconscious.

As he stands above the body, breathing heavily and surrounded by hundreds of natives with looks of shock and anger on their faces, God's voice booms out again and says, "Right... now you're screwed."

* * *

A very religious lady comes back from church one evening and catches a burglar in her house. Unfazed and confident in the power of the Bible, she shouts, "Stop! Acts 2:38!"

The burglar stops dead in his tracks, freezes and drops whatever he had managed to grab. The old lady strides to the telephone and calls the police, who arrive promptly.

"I don't understand," the policeman says to the old lady, as he's clicking the pair of handcuffs shut on the intruder's wrists. "What did you tell him?"

"Acts 2:38. Repent and be baptised, every one of you, in the name of Jesus Christ so that your sins may be forgiven," she explains piously.

"What? I thought she had an axe and two .38s!" exclaims the distraught burglar.

* * *

The Pope is in Great Britain. He's trying to travel incognito and relax a bit in his hired limousine. He watches the British countryside pass by; he sees in the distance the slender spires of country churches, and it makes him feel good. After a couple of hours of that, though, he's getting bored.

He taps the driver the shoulder of and says, "My son, would you indulge an old man in a bit of fun? I've always wanted to drive a big car. Could we swap?"

The driver, not wanting to argue with the pontiff, stops the car and sits at the back.

The Pope is quite happy at the wheel of this huge limousine, which he's driving over the limit – not too much, but just enough to be spotted by a patrol car.

The policeman has a look at him and blanches.

"Sergeant," he says to his superior in the car. "I don't know if we wouldn't be better off forgetting about this incident."

"Why? What's the problem?"

"Well, it looks like we've got a pretty important guy in this car."

"Who is it?"

"I don't know, Sarge. The windows are tinted, but I strongly recommend we get out of here quick."

"Come off it!" the sergeant scoffs. "No one's above the law, not even the Prime Minister."

As the policeman doesn't reply, the sergeant becomes uncertain.

"It's not the Prime Minister, is it?"

"I don't know, Sarge, but this guy's got the Pope as his chauffeur…"

* * *

There were these two priests who rode bicycles to their parish church every week. One day one of the priests shows up to 'work' without his bicycle.

The other priest says to him, "Where's your bike gone Father Michael?"

Father Michael replies, "I'm not really sure, but I think it's been stolen!"

The other priest tells him that, at the next sermon he gives, he should read out the ten commandments, and that when he gets to 'Thou Shalt Not Steal', someone will own up to stealing the bicycle from him.

The next time the two priests see each other, they are both on bicycles again. The other priest asks Father Michael, "So you made the thief own up then did you father?"

Father Michael says, "Well not really, I took your advice sure enough, and I was reading out the Ten Commandments. I got to 'Thou Shalt Not Commit Adultery', when I all of a sudden remembered where I'd left my bike!"

* * *

One Sunday morning, everyone in a bright, beautiful, tiny town gets up early and goes to the local church.

Before the service, the townspeople are sitting in their pews and talking about their lives, their families, etc. when suddenly Satan appears at the front of the church.

Everyone starts screaming and running for the door, trampling one other in a frantic effort to get away from evil incarnate. Soon everyone is evacuated from the church, except for one elderly gentleman who sits calmly in his pew, not moving, seemingly oblivious to the fact that he is in the presence of God's ultimate enemy.

Now, this confuses Satan a bit, so he walks up to the man and says, "Don't you know who I am?"

The man replies, "Yep, sure do."

Satan asks, "Aren't you afraid of me?"

"Nope, sure ain't," says the man.

Satan is a little perturbed at this and asks, "Why aren't you afraid of me?"

The man calmly replies, "Been married to your sister for over 48 years."

* * *

One day in the Garden of Eden, Eve calls out to God, "Lord, I have a problem."

"What's the problem Eve?"

"Lord, I know you've created me and have provided this beautiful garden and all of these wonderful animals, and that hilarious snake, but I'm just not happy."

"Why is that Eve?" came the reply from above.

"Lord, I am lonely, and sick of apples."

"In that case, I shall create a bloke for you."

"What's a bloke, Lord?"

"This bloke will be a flawed creature, with aggressive tendencies, an enormous ego, and an inability to empathise or listen to you properly. All in all, he'll give you a hard time. But, he'll be bigger and faster and more muscular that you. He'll be really good at fighting, kicking a ball and hunting, and not all that bad in the sack."

"Sounds great," says Eve, with a raised brow.

"Yeah well, you can have him on one condition," says God. "Because of his tender ego, you'll have to let him think I made him first. Just remember, it's our little secret… You know, woman to woman."

* * *

A priest is shopping in the local town, when he returns to his car and discovers he has been given a parking ticket. The traffic warden is still writing out the ticket when he arrives.

The priest asks, "Oh, you couldn't waive the ticket could you now, son?"

The traffic warden replies, "Oh father, I'm so sorry, but I've begun to write it, and I'm not allowed to stop halfway through. If you'd just been a minute quicker…"

"Oh well," says the priest, "I'm terrible with parking. I never remember what the time is or where I've parked, to be sure."

"That's very decent of you father," says the traffic warden. "Quite often when this happens, us traffic wardens get given a whole load of abuse."

"Oh my goodness, that's awful," says the priest. "After all, you're only doing your job aren't you? Now, there's a tea party at the abbey this Sunday, would you like to come over?"

"Well father, that's very nice of you to ask, I'd love to. And thanks again for being so understanding," says the traffic warden.

"And perhaps you'd like to bring your father and your mother, too," says the priest. "I could marry the pair of them while I'm at it!"

* * *

A man joins an order of silent monks. He doesn't say a word for ten years. After that time, there is a meal held in his honour and the head monk says to him, "Brother Peter, you have been with us for ten years now, you are permitted to break your vow of silence and to say whatever you'd like to say."

Brother Peter says, "I'd quite like to have some more food in the evenings, please. I've been getting hungry lately."

Another ten years pass, and another meal is held in Brother Peter's honour. The head monk makes a speech.

"Brother Peter, you have been with us for another ten years now, you are permitted to break your vow of silence and to say whatever you'd like to say."

Brother Peter says, "I'd quite like to have some more wine in the evenings, please. I've been getting thirsty lately."

Another ten years pass, and another meal is held in Brother Peter's honour. The head monk makes his customary speech.

"Brother Peter, you have been with us for another ten years now, you are permitted to break your vow of silence and to say whatever you'd like to say."

Brother Peter says, "Father, I think I'm going to leave the order. I don't really think I'm cut out for this life."

"I'm not surprised Brother Peter – you've done nothing but complain since you got here," the father replies.

A drunk staggers into church and manages to make his way into one of the confessionals. He sits there in silence. The priest coughs once to get the man's attention, but the man just ignores him and sits there. The priest can see that the man isn't asleep, so he coughs again, only this time louder. The man still ignores him. The priest then knocks on the divider in a last attempt to get the man to speak.

This seems to have the desired effect, and the man shouts to the priest, "It's no use knocking, there's no paper in this bloody one either!"

* * *

A man is confused about sex and the Sabbath. He just cannot work out whether having sex on the Sabbath is a sin or not, because he doesn't know whether it is work or play. He goes to see his local priest and asks him what his opinion is on this matter. The priest gets his bible down and flicks through it, reading a passage here and a passage there.

Eventually he tells the man, "Well, my son,

after consulting the good book, I have decided that sex is closest to work and that therefore you should not practice it on the Sabbath."

The man thanks the priest but, as that wasn't really the answer he was looking for, he decides to go and see the local minister, who is married and may see things a bit more his way.

He asks the minister the question and, to his disappointment, the minister gives him the same answer as the priest.

"No sex on the Sabbath."

The man decides to go and see another type of holy man – the local Rabbi. The Rabbi is asked the question, and he ponders it over.

Eventually he says, "Well, my son, I have come to the conclusion that sex is definitely play, so therefore you can have sex on the Sabbath."

The man says, "That's great Rabbi, but how do you come to that conclusion when so many others disagree?"

The Rabbi thinks a little and then says quietly, "If sex were work, my wife would get the maid to do it!"

* * *

A man is rushed to his nearest hospital in New York, Our Holy Mother of BeJesus, after a heart attack. The surgeon performs heart surgery, and the man survives no problem. Afterwards, the man is lying in his bed and one of the nuns is comforting him.

"Don't worry sir, you'll be just fine, it's all over now," says the nun. "But we would like to know, sir, if you don't mind the asking, as to how you intend to pay your bill for the operation and the care. Would you be covered by an insurance policy?'

"Well, actually sister, I don't think I am," the man replies.

"Oh dear," continues the nun. "Maybe you've got a load of money lying around and you'd like to pay by cash?"

"Er, no. I don't think so sister," the man replies. "I'm not really a man of much material wealth."

"Well," says the nun, "perhaps you've some close family who could help out?"

"Well not really, sister," the man replies, "I've just the one sister in County Kerry in the old country, but she's a spinster nun."

The nun replies, "Nuns are not spinsters, sir. Nuns are married to God."

"In that case," says the man, "perhaps you could get my brother-in-law to foot the bill!"

STRANDED

A man has been on a desert island for five years. One day, while he was knee deep in the sea spearing a fish, he notices a strange movement in the water. A few minutes later, a few feet away from him, a gorgeous woman in a tight wet suit stands up. Dumbfounded, he simply watches her approaching, dripping with water, teeth flashing, hips swaying.

"How long has it been since you last had a cigarette," she asks in a throaty voice.

"Man, it's been ages," the guy answers in a shaky voice.

The woman diver opens the zip of her breast pocket and fishes out a packet of cigarettes and a lighter. She places a cigarette in his mouth and lights it. She lets the guy take a drag and then asks, "How long has it been since you last had a nice scotch?"

"A long, long time," the guy replies, holding his breath.

The woman pulls down the front zip of her wet suit, just enough to reach down and bring out a bottle of bourbon. She places her hands around the neck and gently twists the cap open. She takes a swig, licks the liquid on her lip and passes the bottle to the guy, and then asks, her finger toying suggestively with her front zip, "Tell me, how long has it been since you last played around?"

"Oh my God," breathes the guy. "Don't tell me you have golf clubs in there too..."

* * *

A man has spent two days in the desert and is now thoroughly parched. On the evening of the third day, he sees a building in the distance. He stumbles along, choking on sand, for another hour and gets to a kind of shop.

"Please, a drink …," he whispers to the man at the door.

"I'm sorry," the man says. "I only sell ties. Can't help you there."

The thirsty guy begs and implores, to no avail. there is no drink to be had.

He plods on and, on the evening of the third day, he sees a building in the distance. He gathers his last bit of energy and crawls towards the lights.

Miracle! Here, in the desert, is a bar! He staggers to the bouncer at the door and croaks, "Mercy… a drink, please…"

"Sorry, mate," the bouncer says, "can't let you in without a tie."

* * *

A farmer is shipwrecked after a big storm and ends up on a desert island with only an Alsatian and a sheep for company. There is enough food for them all, and there is plentiful fresh water, too. The weather is great, and they all have a pretty good time. After a few months, the three of them get into the habit of walking up into the hills to watch the sun go down every evening. One particularly balmy night, everything is just beautiful: the sea can be heard gently lapping in the distance; the cool breeze carries the sound of the crickets chirping; and everyone is happy. The farmer looks over at the sheep and the sheep looks back. They glance into each other's eyes, and the farmer starts to feel warm inside. The sheep continues to look at him, so he reaches out and puts his arm around the animal. As soon as he does this, the Alsatian begins to growl, and doesn't stop until the arm is removed. The three of them continue to watch the sunset, but there is no more funny business.

After a few more weeks there is a huge storm and a beautiful woman is washed up on the beach. She is pretty ill and has to be tended night and day for weeks before she even has enough strength to talk. After a few months of tender, loving care the woman is perfectly well again, and the four of them all get along fine. The farmer, the sheep and the Alsatian introduce the woman to their nightly ritual of watching the sun go down, and one night they are all there and it is just magical. As before, they can hear the sea, smell the scented air and see the most beautiful sunset of their lives, and, as before, romance is most certainly in the air. The farmer is getting his warm feeling inside, so he turns to the beautiful, scantily-clad maiden at his side and nuzzles his mouth up next to her ear.

She tips her head to one side to hear what he has to say, as he whispers, "You wouldn't take the dog for a walk, would you?"

STUPIDITY

A trainee lumberjack went to pick up his equipment from the tool store. The tool store manager gave him a chainsaw.

"Be careful with this," said the manager. "This can cut down six trees an hour."

The trainee came back later in the afternoon.

"There must be something wrong with this," he said, handing back the chainsaw. "It's taken me all day just to cut down one tree."

The tool store manager picked up the chainsaw and pulled the cord to start the motor.

"Hey!" said the trainee. "What's that noise?"

* * *

Why do men keep empty milk bottles in the fridge?
In case anyone wants their coffee black.

* * *

A woman is sitting at the counter in a bar with a glass of vodka with an olive in it. She tries to pick the olive up with the toothpick, but it always eludes her, skidding to the other end of the glass. This futile exercise has been going on for half an hour, when the man next to her, exasperated, snatches the toothpick from her hand and adroitly skewers the olive in one stroke.

"This is how you do it," he says to the woman.

"Big deal," the woman mutters darkly. "I already had him so tired out, he couldn't get away."

* * *

Why did the man ask all his friends to save their burnt-out light bulbs? Because he was trying to build a dark room.

* * *

A woman is sitting alone in a bar, getting bored. A well-dressed bloke, eager for some easy fun, comes up to her and says, "Let's have a game. I'm going to ask you a question. If you can't answer it, you'll give me £5. Then you ask me a question. If I can't answer, I'll give you £50. Is that a deal?"

The woman thinks about it and agrees.

"Here's my question: What's the distance between the Earth and the Moon?"

The woman doesn't even bother to try. She reaches in her purse for a fiver and gives it to the guy.

"OK, my question now," she says. "What's red and blue and jumps all over the place?"

The guy thinks about it for several long minutes but, eventually, he must admit he doesn't have a clue.

Grudgingly, he gives the woman £50, which she pockets with a smile.

"Hold on a minute!" the guy says. "What is red and blue and jumps all over the place?"

The woman looks at him and wordlessly hands him a fiver.

Two men are walking in the beautiful Australian outback. One of them asks the other, "I wonder which is further... London or the Moon?"

The other looks at him in amazement. "Don't be stupid! Can you see London from here?"

* * *

Two dumb guys are standing on a cliff. One of them has a row of budgies attached to his arms; the other has a line of parrots. They both stretch out their arms together and jump.

A day later, in hospital, the first guy tells the second, "Well, I can't say I think much of this budgie-jumping craze."

"Yeah, and I won't go paragliding again ever."

* * *

Three women go to a funfair and buy a raffle ticket. As it's for charity, everyone wins a small prize. The first woman wins a case of spaghetti sauce. The second wins a small Stilton cheese. The third wins a toilet brush.

The following day, they meet at the first woman's place and she says, "Wasn't that great? I love spaghetti!"

"And I adore cheese," comments the second woman, then asks the third, "How's the toilet brush?"

"Not so good, I'm afraid," she answers. "In fact, I think I'll go back to paper."

* * *

A man walks up to the counter of the local library and complains to the librarian. "Here's your book back. It's the most boring book I have ever read. There's no plot whatsoever, and far too many characters."

"Oh, thank you," the librarian replies. "You must be the person who borrowed our phone book."

* * *

A man goes into a shop and sees something he doesn't recognise.

He asks the assistant what it is. The assistant replies, "That's a Thermos flask. It keeps hot things hot and cold things cold."

Amazed by this incredible invention, the man buys it immediately. He walks into work the next day with his new Thermos.

His boss sees him and asks, "What's that shiny object?"

"It keeps hot things hot and cold things cold," says the man, proudly.

The boss asks, "What do you have in it?"

"Two cups of tea and a choc ice," the man replies.

TRAVEL

The first mate on a ship decided to celebrate his birthday with some contraband rum. Unfortunately, he was still drunk the next morning. Realising this, the captain wrote in the ship's log: "The first mate was drunk today."

"Captain, please don't let that stay in the log," the mate said. "This could add months or years to my becoming a captain myself."

"Is it true?" asked the captain, already knowing the answer.

"Yes, it's true," the mate said.

"Then, if it's true, it has to go in the log. That's the rule," said the captain, sternly.

A few weeks later, it was the first mate's turn to make the log entries. The first mate wrote: "The ship seems in particularly good shape. The captain was sober today."

* * *

Dave says to Phil, "You know, I reckon I'm about ready for a holiday, only this year I'm gonna do it a little different. The last few years, I took your advice as to where to go. Two years ago, you said to go to Tenerife; I went to Tenerife, and Marie got pregnant. Then last year you told me to go to the Bahamas; I went to the Bahamas, and Marie got pregnant again."

Phil says, "So what are you gonna do different this year?"

Dave says, "This year, I'm takin' Marie with me..."

A man and a woman end up having to share a sleeping car, thanks to the unfathomable powers of the Virgin Trains booking system. They do not know one another and are quite shy at first, but after a while a kind of consensus is found; the man is going to sleep on the top bunk, while the woman is going to sleep at the bottom.

All goes well, and they are snugly lying in their separate beds when the man says, "Excuse me, miss, but can you reach the drawer where they keep the extra blankets? I'd do it myself, but I didn't want to disturb you by climbing down."

The woman, who is just starting to fall asleep, wakes up with a start. She grumbles, but eventually gets out of bed and passes the guy an extra blanket. She goes back to sleep, only to be woken up a few minutes later.

"Excuse me, it's me again," the guy says rather lamely.

"Could you pass me another pillow from the same cupboard?"

The woman takes a deep breath and replies, "I'll tell you what. Seeing as we're getting on quite well together, and we've got to share this car together, why don't we act as if we were actually together, like husband and wife?"

"Sure, that'd be great," the man agrees, a sudden vision of acrobatic sex flashing through his mind.

"Good," the woman purrs. Then she yells, "Now get your lazy ass down and get your pillow yourself, asshole!"

* * *

Two American tourists were travelling through Wales. As they approached Llangollen, they started arguing about the pronunciation of the town's name until they stopped for lunch.

As they stood waiting for their food, one tourist asked the counter assistant, "Excuse me, miss. Could you settle an argument for us? Would you please pronounce where we are very slowly?"

The counter assistant leans over and says, "Burrrrrrr Gurrrrrr Kingggg."

* * *

A man is flying on a four-engine plane. Suddenly, there's a loud bang. The pilot comes on the radio and says, "I'm sorry, but we seem to have lost an engine. We'll probably be delayed by 45 minutes."

A few minutes later, there's another bang. Once again, the radio comes on. "I'm sorry, but we seem to have lost another engine. We'll probably be delayed by two hours."

A little while later, the third engine shuts off. This time, the pilot tells the passengers that they will be delayed by around three hours.

The man turns to the guy sitting beside him and says, "Man, if they lose the fourth engine, we'll be up here all day."

* * *

A jumbo jet is just coming into the airport on its final approach. The pilot comes on the intercom, "This is your Captain. We're on our final descent. I want to thank you for flying with us today, and I hope you enjoy your stay."

But he forgets to switch off the intercom. Now

the whole plane can hear his conversation from the cockpit.

The co-pilot says to the pilot, "Well skipper, what are you going to do in town?"

Now all ears are listening to this conversation.

"Well," says the skipper, "first I'm going to check into the hotel and have a beer in the bar. Then I'm going take that new stewardess out for supper; you know, the one with the great legs. I'm going to wine and dine her, then take her back to my room for an all-night marathon session."

Everyone on the plane is trying to get a look at the new stewardess. Mortally embarrassed, she runs from the back of the plane to try and get to the cockpit to turn the intercom off. Halfway down the aisle, she trips over an old lady's bag and falls over.

The old lady leans down, pats her shoulder kindly and says, "No need to run, dear. He's going to have a beer first."

A man walks into a pub with his wife. His wife sits down while he orders drinks, and a friend of his at the bar asks him where he's been.

"On holiday," he replies.

"Where on holiday?" his friend asks.

"Spain."

"Whereabouts in Spain?"

"Some little village on the coast."

"What's it called?"

"I forget. What's the name of that plant that grows up the sides of houses?"

"Ivy."

"That's it," he says, then shouts, "Ivy, what's the name of the village we stayed at in Spain?"

* * *

A man is on a low-budget flight to Amsterdam, waiting for takeoff. Another bloke comes up and says, "Excuse me, but you're in my seat."

"Don't think so. First come, first served with this airline, mate," responds the man, remaining seated.

"Look here," the newcomer insists, "I fly to Amsterdam every day, and I sit in that seat every day! Now, do I have to go and get a flight attendant?"

"Get whoever you want," shrugs the seated man. Annoyed, the other man disappears for a short while and returns with a flight attendant. "I'm sorry, sir, but I'm going to have to ask you to choose another seat," she says. The man stands up, picks up his bag in a huff and says, "Fine. I didn't want to fly the plane anyway!"

* * *

Two blokes go on holiday together, and while Sam
has great success with the ladies, Ken gets nowhere.

"How can I impress the chicks like you?" asks
Ken.

Sam gives him a potato, telling him that if he
puts it in his trunks he can't fail. But after an hour
of parading up and down the beach Ken gets
disillusioned because he still hasn't pulled.

"It's no good, the potato trick hasn't worked,"
says Ken in a sulk.

Sam can barely contain his laughter when he
spots the problem, "No. You were meant to put it
down the *front* of your trunks!"

* * *

An American tourist in Dublin decides to duck
out of his tour group and explore the city on his
own. He wanders around, taking in the sights and
occasionally stopping at a quaint pub to soak up
the local culture, chat with the lads and have a
pint of Guinness. After a while, he finds himself

in a very high-class area: big, stately residences, no pubs, no shops, no restaurants and, worst of all, no public toilets. He really needs to go after all those pints of Guinness and manages to find a narrow side-street – the perfect solution to his problem. As he's unzipping, he's tapped on the shoulder by a policeman, who says, "I say, sir, you simply cannot do that here, you know."

"I'm very sorry, officer," replies the American, "but I really, really have to go, and I just can't find a public toilet."

"Ah, yes," says the policeman. "Just follow me." He leads him to a back delivery alley, then along a wall to a gate, which he opens. "In there," points the policeman. "Whizz away, sir. Anywhere you want."

The fellow enters and finds himself in the most beautiful garden he has ever seen: manicured grass lawns, statues, fountains, sculptured hedges and huge beds of gorgeous flowers, all in perfect bloom.

Since he has the policeman's blessing, he unburdens himself and is greatly relieved. As he goes back through the gate, he says to the policeman, "That was really decent of you. Is that your famed Irish hospitality?"

"No, sir," replies the cop. "That's what we call the British Embassy."

WORK

**What's the difference between a mechanic
and a herd of elephants?
The mechanic charges more.**

* * *

An old nun who lives in a convent next to a construction site notices the bad language of the workers, and decides to spend some time with them to correct their ways.

She decides she'll take her lunch, sit with the workers and talk with them. So she puts her sandwich in a brown bag and walks over to the spot where the men are eating. She walks up to the group and with a big smile says, "Do you men know Jesus Christ?"

They shake their heads and look at each other. One of the workers looks up into the steelwork and yells, "Anybody up there know Jesus Christ?"

One of the steelworkers shouts, "Why?"

The worker yells back, "His wife's here with his lunch."

* * *

A bloke goes before a judge to try to get excused from jury service, and the judge asks him why he can't serve as a juror.

"I don't want to be away from my job for that long," replies the bloke.

"Can't they do without you at work?" asks the judge.

"Yes," says the bloke. "But I don't want them to know it."

* * *

A young businessman is leaving the office late one night when he finds his boss standing over the shredder with a piece of paper in his hand.

"This is a very sensitive official document," says the boss. "My secretary's gone for the night. Can you make this thing work?"

"Sure," says the keen underling, as he takes the paper, puts it in the shredder and hits the start button.

"Great," says his boss. "I just need the one copy, thanks."

* * *

A guy walks into a watchmaker's shop and asks the man behind the counter for a potato clock.

"A potato clock?" says the watchmaker, "I've never heard of a potato clock. Why do you want one?"

The customer sighs. "Well, you see," he says, "I went for a job interview yesterday and was offered the job. So I asked the boss what time I should start, and he said nine o'clock."

"So?" asks the kindly old shopkeeper.

"Well," replies the man, "he said to do that, I'll need to get a potato clock."

* * *

A man was passing a country estate and saw a sign on the gate.

It read: "Please ring bell for the caretaker." He rang the bell and an old man appeared.

"Are you the caretaker?" the fellow asked.

"Yes, I am," replied the old man. "What do you want?"

"I'd just like to know why you can't ring the bell yourself."

* * *

One of the main host computers of a very busy internal network went down, bringing down with it half the intranet of the building which depended on it. The network in-house engineer soon gave up and told his boss to call for a specialist.

The specialist arrived, had a talk with the engineer, then took one look at the computer and nodded thoughtfully. He then opened his briefcase, produced a small rubber hammer and, his ear stuck to the computer case, hit a spot softly, after which the system did a kind of 'Wooosh' noise and restarted straight away.

Two days later the office manager received a bill from the consultant for £2,000.

Immediately he called the engineer's agency and exclaimed, "Two thousand pounds for fixing that computer? You were only here five minutes! I want the bill itemized!"

The next day the new bill arrived. It read:
'Tapping computer with hammer: £1
Knowing where to tap: £1,999'.

* * *

Resolving to surprise her husband, an executive's wife stops by his office. When she opens the door, she finds him with his secretary sitting in his lap.

Without hesitating, he dictates, "...And in conclusion, gentlemen, budget cuts or no budget cuts, I cannot continue to operate this office with just one chair."

* * *

An office manager arrives at his department and sees an employee sitting behind his desk, totally stressed out.

He gives him a spot of advice, "I went home every afternoon for two weeks and had myself pampered by my wife. It was fantastic, and it really helped me. Maybe you should give it a try, too."

Two weeks later, when the manager arrives at his department, he sees the same man happy and full of energy at his desk. The faxes are piling up, and the computer is running at full speed.

"Excellent," says the manager, "I see you followed my advice."

"I did," answers the employee. "It was great! By the way, I didn't know you had such a nice house!"

* * *

Three women all work at the same office for a female boss who always goes home early.

"Hey, girls," says the first, "let's go home early tomorrow. She'll never know." So the next day, they all leave right after the boss does.

The first woman gets some extra gardening done, the second woman goes to a bar, and the third woman goes home to find her husband having sex with the female boss! She quietly sneaks out of the house, and then later returns home at her more normal time. The next morning at work, they discuss the previous afternoon.

"That was fun," says the first woman.

"We should do it again sometime," says the second.

"No way," says the third. "I almost got caught."

A boy goes to the Jobcentre and says, "I'd like to work in a bowling alley."

"Ten pin?" says the man behind the desk.

"No, permanent," says the boy.